Quilts
for All
Seasons

Compiled by Susan Ramey Wright
Edited by Patricia Wilens

OXMOOR HOUSE®

Contents

Quilts for All Seasons
from the *For the Love of Quilting* series

© 1993 by Oxmoor House, Inc.
Book Division of Southern Progress Corporation
P.O. Box 2463, Birmingham, Alabama 35201
Published by Oxmoor House, Inc., and Leisure Arts, Inc.

Library of Congress Number: 93-083737
Hardcover ISBN: 0-8487-1109-2
Softcover ISBN: 0-8487-1176-9
Manufactured in the United States of America
First Printing 1993

Editor-in-Chief: Nancy J. Fitzpatrick
Senior Crafts Editor: Susan Ramey Wright
Senior Editor, Editorial Services: Olivia Kindig Wells
Director of Manufacturing: Jerry Higdon
Art Director: James Boone

Quilts for All Seasons

Editor: Patricia Wilens
Copy Chief: Mary Jean Haddin
Copy Editor: Susan Smith Cheatham
Editorial Assistant: Roslyn Oneille Hardy
Designer: Melissa Jones Clark
Patterns and Illustrations: Karen Tindall Tillery
Assistant Art Director: Cynthia R. Cooper
Senior Photographer: John O'Hagan
Photostylist: Katie Stoddard
Copy Assistant: Leslee Rester Johnson
Production Manager: Rick Litton
Associate Production Manager: Theresa L. Beste
Production Assistant: Marianne Jordan
Senior Production Designer: Larry Hunter
Publishing Systems Administrator: Rick Tucker
Contributing Photographers: Mary-Gray Hunter,
 Melissa Springer

Spring

Summer

Autumn

Winter

Workshop

Introduction

To everything there is a season, and a time to every purpose under heaven.

Ecclesiastes 3:1

Quiltmakers have long been inspired by the wondrous variety of nature, striving to capture the essence of a beloved flower or tree with the color, pattern, and texture of fabric.

The palette of the changing seasons is reflected in this collection of delightful quilts for you to make. Create spring rainbows, summer fireworks, autumn leaves, and winter snows—using fabric and stitches to hold fond memories of favorite seasons in your heart and mind throughout the year.

A quiltmaker's purpose in any season is to produce something of warmth and beauty. You can extend a quilt's purpose to encompass a heritage of pride and continuity by signing and dating it. Instead of the mysteries left in our forebears' anonymous quilts, make yours a quilt for all times, for all times are the seasons of heaven.

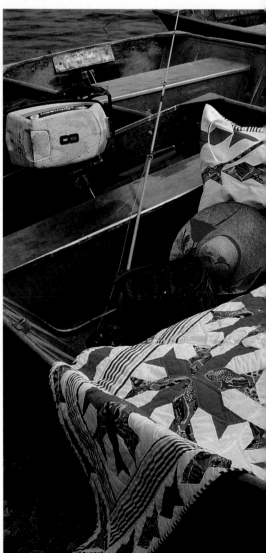

Rules of Thumb

Here are a few things to keep in mind when making the quilts in this collection. For more detailed quiltmaking information, turn to the Workshop chapter, which begins on page 142.

• Fabric requirements are based on 44"/45"-wide fabric and allow for up to 4% shrinkage.

• 100% cotton fabric is recommended for both the quilt top and for backing.

• Wash, dry, and press all fabrics before cutting.

• Materials are listed to make each quilt as shown. Select fabrics in the colors of your choice in the quantities stated. If you want to change the finished size of the quilt, adjust yardage as needed.

• Read all instructions for the selected project before you begin to cut.

• Cut pieces from each fabric in the order in which they are listed, cutting largest pieces first. This ensures efficient use of the yardage.

• All seam allowances are ¼" unless otherwise noted.

• All patchwork patterns and measurements for pieces, sashing, and borders include seam allowances. The points on triangle patterns are trimmed so your pieces should fit together perfectly whether you sew by hand or by machine.

• Appliqué patterns are drawn finished size and do not include seam allowances. Add a ¼" seam allowance around each piece when cutting appliqué pieces from fabric.

• Determine size of batting needed from finished size of quilt.

• For most full-size quilts, backing is made by joining two widths of fabric that are the length of the quilt plus 4" for hand quilting or plus 8" for machine quilting. Larger quilts may require three widths. Quilts less than 40" wide require only one width of fabric.

• Unless otherwise specified, prepare your quilt for quilting by layering backing (right side down), batting, and top (right side up). Pin or baste the layers together, working from the center out, before quilting.

Spring

Old Mother Earth woke up from her sleep,
　And found she was cold and bare;
The Winter was over, the Spring was near,
　And she had not a dress to wear.
"Alas!" she sighed, with great dismay,
　"Oh, where shall I get my clothes?
There's not a place to buy a suit,
　And a dressmaker no one knows."
"I'll make you a dress," said springing
　Grass, just looking above the ground,
"A dress of green of the loveliest sheen,
　To cover you all around."
"And we," said the dandelions gay,
　"Will dot it with yellow bright."
"I'll make a fringe," said forget-me-not,
　"Of blue, very soft and light. . ."
Old Mother Earth was thankful and glad,
　As she put on her dress so gay;
And that is the reason, my little ones,
　She is looking so lovely today.

　　　　　　　Anonymous, "A Spring Song"

Flowers are the hallmark of spring's quilts, a lovely bouquet of pastel fabrics in petal pink, buttery yellow, sky blue, and freshest green. When April showers and May flowers dwindle under the sun's heat, these quilts keep our time-honored love of flowers forever garden-fresh.

Irish Crosses

Finished Size
Blocks: 64 blocks, 12" square
Quilt: 96" x 96"

Materials
2¼ yards of green-on-white print fabric for center
  squares
Scraps or 25 (18" x 22") pieces of assorted light green
  print fabrics
Scraps or 25 (18" x 22") pieces of assorted dark green
  print fabrics
1 yard of binding fabric
8¾ yards of backing fabric (or 3 yards of 108"-wide
  sheeting)

Cutting
Note: Cutting instructions for triangles differ for traditional and quick piecing. Directions for cutting triangles are given with instructions for each technique.

For background squares, cut 11 (6½" x 42") strips across width of green-on-white print fabric. From these, cut 64 (6½") squares.

Traditional Piecing
Scrap savers will love piecing all the triangles in this quilt one pair at a time for a completely scrappy look. Each block has 24 light triangles and 24 dark ones, pieced around a center square.

1. See page 145 for tips on making templates. Make template for Triangle A. Cut 1,536 As each from light green scraps and dark green scraps.

2. Follow Block Assembly diagram to make 4 pieced triangle segments for each block, arranging light and dark triangles as shown.

Block Assembly

3. Sew bottom of each segment to a background square; then stitch diagonal corner seams to join segments. Make 64 blocks.

Quick Piecing
If you're looking for a time-saver, here's a shortcut to reduce marking, cutting, and sewing time. For these blocks, half the triangles can be quick-pieced.

1. Cut all green fabrics in half to get 100 (11" x 18") pieces. From these, select 24 light pieces and 24 darks. From each, cut 8 (4¼") squares. Cut each square in quarters diagonally for a total of 768 light triangles and 768 dark ones. Set aside until time to assemble blocks.

2. Select 2 fabrics from remaining 26 pieces of light fabric. On wrong side of 1 piece, draw a 3 x 5-square grid of 3" squares. Draw diagonal lines through each square as shown in Triangle-Square Grid diagram.

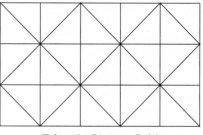

Triangle-Square Grid

3. Layer both fabrics with right sides facing and with marked grid faceup. Pin fabrics together at corners and centers, avoiding diagonal lines.

4. Following directions for half-square triangles on page 149, machine-stitch grids. Cut grid apart to make 30 triangle-squares.

5. Repeat steps 2–4 to mark and stitch grids on 12 more light fabric pairs and 13 dark pairs.

6. Follow Block Assembly diagram to join triangle-squares and individual triangles into 2 light and 2 dark pieced segments for each block.

7. Sew bottom of each segment to a background square; then stitch diagonal corner seams to join segments. Make 64 blocks.

Quilt Top Assembly
Follow Quilt Assembly diagram on page 10 to arrange blocks in 8 horizontal rows of 8 blocks each, matching dark edges to dark edges and light edges to light edges. Stitch blocks in rows; then join rows.

Salute St. Patrick's Day and the new spring with a fabulous scrap quilt. Whether it celebrates the wearing o' the green or any other color, Irish Crosses is easy to make with either traditional or quick piecing techniques.

Quilting and Finishing

Outline-quilt patchwork as shown in Block Quilting diagram. See page 157 for instructions on making and applying binding.

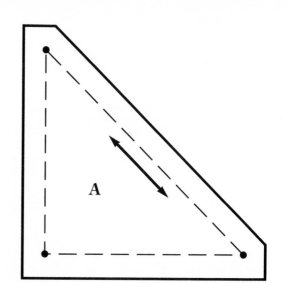

A

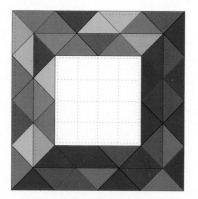

Block Quilting

Quilt Assembly

Butterfly Crib Quilt

Butterflies emerge from cocoons as spring bursts forth from winter, fluttering on late March's gentle breezes. Buttonhole embroidery is used to appliqué the shapes of this pretty pink crib quilt.

Butterfly Crib Quilt

Finished Size

Blocks: 20 blocks, 9¼" square
Quilt: 37" x 46¼"

Materials

1½ yards of white solid fabric
1 yard of pink solid fabric (includes binding)
¼ yard each of 2 pink print fabrics
1½ yards of backing fabric
1 skein of green embroidery floss
2 skeins of pink embroidery floss

Cutting

1. See page 145 for tips on making templates. Make finished-size templates for appliqué patterns A and B. Follow directions for patchwork templates to make a template of Triangle C.

2. Cut 2 (10½" x 42") strips across width of pink solid fabric. Cut 1 strip into 4 (10½") squares; then cut 1 more square from second strip. Cut 4 Cs from each square.

3. Cut white fabric into 2 (10½" x 42") strips and 2 (9¾" x 42") strips. From these, cut 20 Cs as for pink fabric and 10 (9¾") squares for appliquéd blocks.

4. On right side of each print fabric, trace 5 As and 5 Bs with template faceup and 5 more of each with template facedown. Adding seam allowances, cut appliqué pieces for 10 butterflies.

Embroidery and Appliqué

This little quilt is a charming example of buttonhole appliqué—an easy-to-do combination of appliqué and embroidery. If you prefer, it can be made with any other appliqué technique.

1. Fold each background square in half vertically and

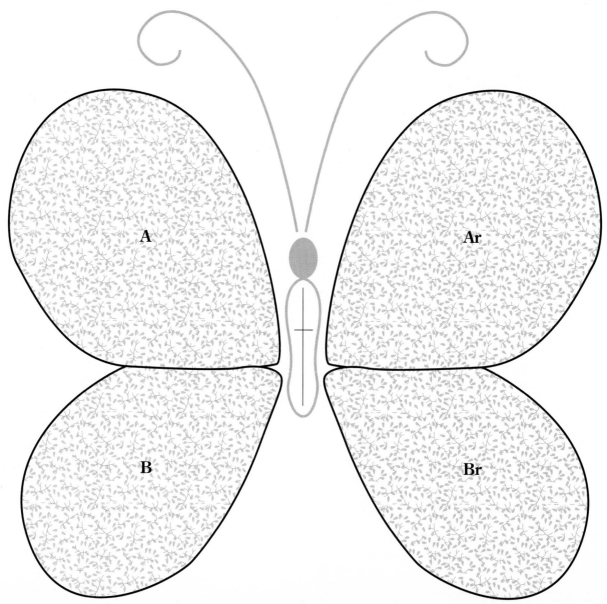

Piecing

1. Join a pink C triangle to each white C, matching short legs to form a large pieced triangle. Press seam allowances toward pink fabric.

2. Join 2 pieced triangles to make a square, offsetting colors as shown in photograph. Make 10 squares.

Quilt Top Assembly

Refer to photograph to arrange blocks in 5 horizontal rows, positioning butterflies of the same fabric in diagonal lines. Join blocks in rows; then join rows.

Quilting and Finishing

Outline-quilt seam lines and butterfly wings.

Use remaining pink solid fabric to make straight-grain binding. See page 157 for instructions on making and applying binding.

horizontally, finger-pressing folds to establish placement guidelines.

2. Position each square over butterfly pattern on opposite page, matching center of fabric with marked center on pattern. Lightly trace embroidery details and wing outlines.

3. Using 2 strands of green floss, work butterfly bodies and antennae in outline stitch. Satin-stitch head.

4. Turn under seam allowance on A and A reversed pieces. Pin in place on background squares, aligning edges with traced outlines.

5. To appliqué, use 2 strands of pink floss to work small buttonhole stitches around edges of each A piece.

6. Appliqué B and B reversed pieces in same manner.

C

Hosanna

Finished Size
Blocks: 15 blocks, 16" square
Quilt: 71¾" x 83¾"

Materials
6 yards of muslin
2 yards of green small print fabric
1⅞ yards of green large print fabric
5 yards of backing fabric (or 2¼ yards of 90"-wide sheeting)

Cutting
1. See page 145 for tips on making templates. Make templates for patterns A–G.
2. Cut 42 (2¾" x 43") crossgrain muslin strips. From these, cut 72 each of C, C reversed, E, E reversed, G, and G reversed. Keep reversed pieces separated from the others.
3. For muslin borders, cut 2 (2½" x 81") strips and 2 (2¾" x 73") strips.
4. Cut 2 (24") muslin squares. Cut these squares into quarters diagonally to make 5 (and 3 extra) setting triangles. Cut 1 of the extras in half to make 2 corner triangles.
5. Cut a 24" x 33" muslin piece. From this, cut 52 (3½") squares for prairie points.
6. Cut 144 As from remaining muslin.
7. Cut 9 (3⅛" x 42") strips of large print fabric. From these, cut 72 Bs and 72 Bs reversed.
8. Cut 12 (3⅛" x 42") strips of large print fabric. From these, cut 72 Ds and 72 Ds reversed.
9. Cut 18 (3⅛" x 36") strips of small print fabric. From these, cut 72 Fs and 72 Fs reversed.
10. From remaining small print fabric, cut 52 (3½") squares for prairie points.

Piecing
1. Referring to Block Piecing diagram, join pieces A, B, C, D, E, F, and G to make a half-square as shown. Use reversed pieces to make the opposite half-square. Press all seam allowances toward darker fabric. Join halves to complete 1 square.

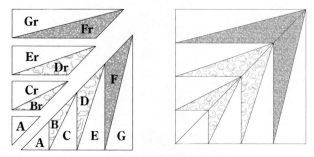

Block Piecing

2. Join 4 squares as shown in Block Assembly diagram to make 1 Hosanna block. Make 15 blocks.

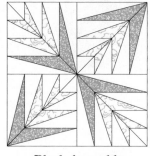

Block Assembly

3. Refer to Half-Block Assembly diagram to make 6 half-blocks.

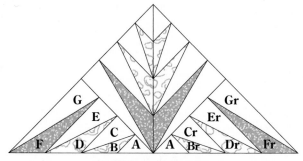

Half-Block Assembly

Quilt Top Assembly
1. Follow Quilt Assembly diagram on page 16 to join blocks, half-blocks, setting triangles, and corner triangles in diagonal rows. If setting triangles are too big, trim to match Hosanna blocks. Join rows.
2. Add a 2½" x 81" border to each long side of quilt. Trim borders even with quilt top. Join remaining borders to top and bottom of quilt.

A theme of Easter is reflected in this palmlike design, appropriately named Hosanna. The narrow-pointed pieces of this patchwork call for careful and skilled piecing.

Quilting and Finishing

Outline-quilt patchwork. Quilt 2" cross-hatching in setting triangles and corner triangles. Quilt borders as desired.

See page 23 for tips on making prairie points and hemming the quilt. Alternating colors as shown in photograph, space 24 prairie points across top and bottom edges and 28 prairie points along each side.

Combine the pastel colors of spring flowers and Easter eggs with quick and easy piecing techniques to make this dramatic patchwork quilt.

Card Tricks

Finished Size

Blocks: 20 blocks, 12" square
Quilt: 70" x 84"

Materials

2¼ yards of pastel green striped fabric for inner border
2 yards of pastel peach striped fabric for outer border
1¾ yards of white solid fabric for blocks
1¾ yards of pastel peach solid fabric for sashing and binding
1¼ yards each of 4 print fabrics (blue, pink, green, peach)
5 yards of backing fabric

Cutting

Note: Cutting instructions for some pieces differ for traditional piecing and quick piecing. The following instructions are for those pieces that are cut the same way for both methods. Additional cutting instructions are given with directions for each technique.

1. For borders, cut 4 (2½" x 71") strips of peach striped fabric and 4 (4½" x 80") strips of green striped fabric.
2. Set aside ⅝ yard of peach solid fabric for binding. From remaining peach fabric, cut 3 (12½" x 43") strips. Then cut these strips into 2½"-wide pieces to make 49 (2½" x 12½") sashing strips.
3. Cut a 4½" x 42" strip from each print fabric. From each strip, cut 1 (4½") square and 11 (2½") squares for borders and sashing.

Traditional Piecing

1. See page 145 for tips on making templates. Make templates for triangles A and B.
2. Cut 80 As and 80 Bs from white fabric.
3. From each print fabric, cut 40 As and 40 Bs.
4. Follow Block Assembly diagram to make 9 pieced squares from white and print triangles. Join squares in horizontal rows; then join rows. Make 20 blocks.

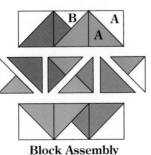

Block Assembly

Quick Piecing

If you're short of time or if marking and cutting just aren't your thing, take a shortcut to reduce the marking, cutting, and sewing time. For these blocks, all triangle pairs can be quick-pieced. See page 148 for more instructions on sewing quick-pieced triangles.

1. Cut 4 (14" x 30") lengthwise strips and 4 (7" x 30") strips from white fabric.
2. From each print fabric, cut 1 (14" x 30") lengthwise strip, 2 (7" x 30") strips, and 10 (4⅞") squares. Cut squares in half diagonally to make 20 A triangles.
3. On the wrong side of each 14" x 30" white piece, draw a 2 x 5-square grid of 4⅞" squares. Draw diagonal lines through each square as shown in Triangle-Square Grid A.

Triangle-Square Grid A

4. Match each white piece with a same-size print fabric piece, with right sides facing and marked grid faceup. Pin fabrics together at corners and centers, avoiding diagonal lines.
5. Following directions for half-square triangles on page 149, machine-stitch grids. Cut grids apart to make 20 A/A triangle-squares from each grid.
6. On wrong side of each 7" x 30" white piece, draw a 1 x 5-square grid of 5¼" squares. Draw diagonal lines through these as shown in Triangle-Square Grid B.

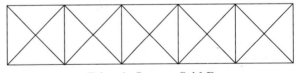

Triangle-Square Grid B

7. Match and pin marked white pieces to print fabrics as before. (You will have 1 piece of each print fabric leftover.) Following directions for quarter-square triangles on page 149, machine-stitch grids. Cut 20 B/B half-square triangles from each grid.
8. Repeat steps 6 and 7 to make 20 B/B blue/pink half-square triangles and 20 B/B green/peach half-square triangles.

9. Follow Block Assembly diagram to make 9 pieced squares for each block. Join squares in horizontal rows; then join rows. Make 20 blocks.

Quilt Top Assembly

1. Referring to Quilt Assembly diagram, arrange blocks in 5 horizontal rows of 4 blocks each with sashing strips between. Join blocks and sashing strips in each row. Add sashing strips to ends of rows. Press seam allowances toward sashing.

Quilt Assembly

2. To make each horizontal sashing row, join 5 print squares and 4 sashing strips as shown. Distribute colors of sashing squares as desired. Make 6 rows. Press seam allowances toward sashing strips.

3. Follow Quilt Assembly diagram to join block rows and sashing rows.

4. Stitch a sashing square to 1 end of a green border strip. Compare length of border strip to side of quilt top and trim the unstitched end as necessary, allowing for another sashing square and seam allowance. Add sashing square to trimmed end; then press seam allowances toward squares. Join borders to sides of quilt top.

5. Add borders to top and bottom edges in same manner, adding 2 sashing squares at both ends of each border strip.

6. Join peach borders to sides. Trim borders even with quilt top. For top and bottom, add 4½" print squares to both ends of remaining border strips as before and join borders to quilt top.

Quilting and Finishing

Quilt patchwork as shown in Block Quilting diagram. Quilt sashing and borders as desired. See page 157 for instructions on making and applying binding.

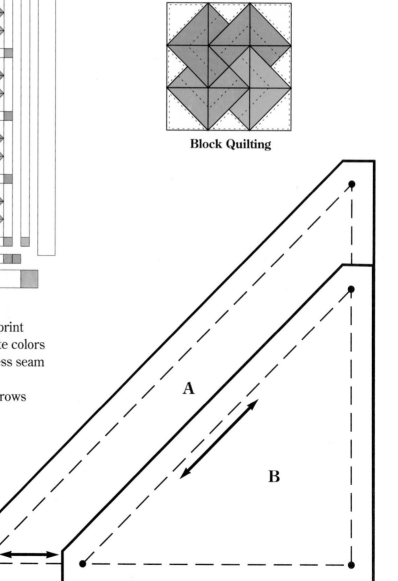

Block Quilting

Noah's Star Crib Quilt

March winds go out like a lamb, making way for April showers. Remember the deluge with embroidered beasts from the biblical tale, framed in rainbow patchwork.

Noah's Star Crib Quilt

Finished Size
Blocks: 4 blocks, 18" square
Quilt: 58" x 58"

Materials
2 yards of blue solid fabric
1¾ yards of rainbow-striped fabric
1¾ yards of white solid fabric
3¼ yards of backing fabric
4 skeins of blue embroidery floss
Tracing paper (optional)

Cutting
1. See page 145 for tips on making templates. Make templates of patterns A and B.
2. Cut 20 (10") squares of white fabric. (These are cut oversized for easy handling while embroidering.)
3. Cut 2 (7½" x 42") strips across width of blue fabric and 1 strip from both striped and white fabrics. Cut 16 Bs from each strip.
4. From blue fabric, cut 2 (6½" x 19") strips and 1 (6½" x 43") strip for sashing. Cut 2 (6¾" x 43") strips and 2 (6¾" x 55") strips for borders.

Embroidery
1. Trace 1 embroidery pattern onto each white square, centering design on fabric. Trace 1 each of Noah, ark, sun, and dove designs. Trace 1 of each animal with pattern faceup and 1 of each animal with pattern facedown to make mirror-image sets.
2. Using 3 strands of floss, embroider all traced lines in outline stitch. Make eyes and other details with satin stitch or French knots, if desired. Remove any visible markings. Lightly press blocks.

Piecing
1. Center Template A on each embroidered block; trim excess fabric. If you prefer, use an acrylic ruler with a rotary cutter instead of the template to trim blocks.
2. Join white triangles to blue triangles, matching short sides as shown in Diagram 1. Join striped triangles and remaining blue triangles in the same manner. Press all seam allowances toward blue fabric.

Diagram 1

3. Following Diagram 1, join 2 triangle pairs to make a pieced square. Make 16 squares.
4. Arrange 4 pieced squares with 5 embroidered squares, referring to photograph for placement. Note that each block has the same animal in opposite corners. Join squares to complete each block.

Quilt Top Assembly
1. Join 2 blocks with a 19" sashing strip between them. Repeat for remaining 2 blocks. Press seam allowances toward sashing. Trim sashing even with blocks.
2. Stitch the 2 sections together with 43" sashing strip between them.
3. Sew border strips to top and bottom edges; then add side borders.

Quilting
1. See page 153 for tips on making stencils of quilting patterns X and Y on page 29.
2. Referring to photograph, position Stencil X on outer borders and sashing. Mark clamshell design, adjusting stencil position at corners as necessary. Mark Stencil Y on center sashing, adjusting stencil position as necessary to connect rainbow lines at the intersection of sashing strips.
3. Quilt on all marked lines. In blocks, outline-quilt ¼" from each seam line.

B

Prairie Points

1. Cut 80 (5") squares from striped fabric.

2. Following Diagram 2, fold each square in half twice to make a small triangle. Press.

3. With right sides facing and raw edges aligned, pin 16 to 18 prairie points to each quilt top edge.

Space prairie points evenly, starting at a corner and overlapping adjacent points as shown in Diagram 3.

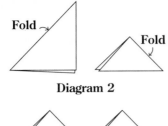

Fold

Fold

Diagram 2

Diagram 3

4. When satisfied with spacing, sew prairie points in place with a ½" seam (Diagram 4).

5. Press prairie points to right side. Trim batting if necessary. Fold under a ½" hem on backing to cover raw edges of prairie points. Blindstitch in place (Diagram 5).

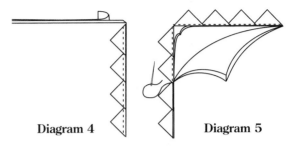

Diagram 4

Diagram 5

A

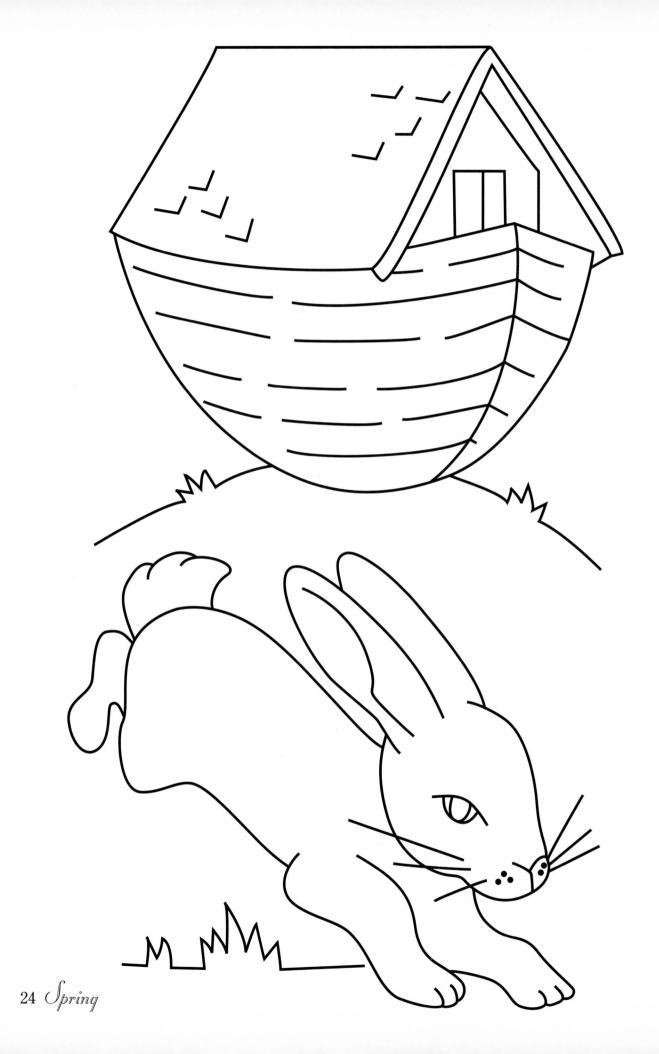

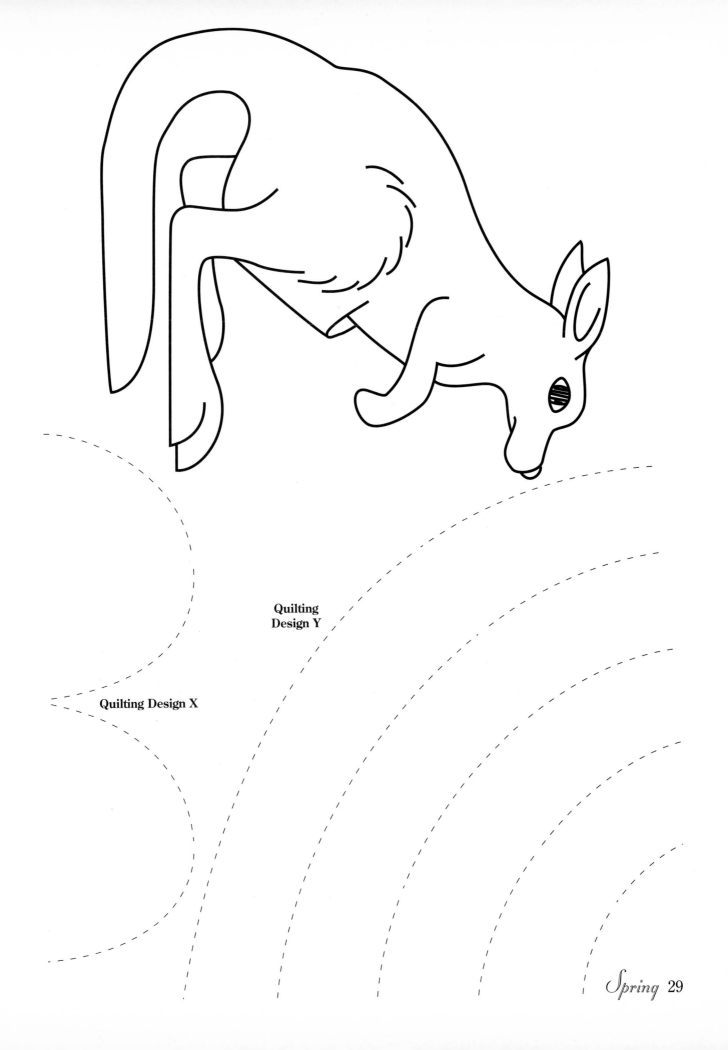

Quilting
Design Y

Quilting Design X

Dutch Treat

Finished Size
Blocks: 45 blocks, 6" x 10"
Quilt: 66" x 82"

Materials
2½ yards of floral print fabric for outer border
   and binding
2¼ yards of yellow print fabric for sashing and
   inner border
2⅛ yards of sky blue fabric
1 yard of green print fabric for leaves and stems
¼ yard each of 5 light solid fabrics for tulips
⅛ yard each or scraps of 5 coordinating dark solid
   fabrics for tulip centers
5 yards of backing fabric

Cutting
Note: The following instructions are for all pieces except
A triangles, which are cut differently for traditional piecing and quick piecing. Cutting instructions for As are
given with directions for each technique.

1. See page 145 for tips on making templates. Make
templates for patterns D and K. For patterns A, B, C, E,
and G, make templates or use an acrylic ruler with a
rotary cutter to measure and cut pieces as follows.
2. Cut 9 (1⅞") squares from each dark solid fabric to
make 45 Bs.
3. Cut 2 (3¼" x 42") strips of sky blue fabric. From
these, cut 23 (3¼") squares. Cut each square in quarters
diagonally to make 90 C triangles.
4. Cut 2 (5" x 42") strips of sky blue fabric. From these,
cut 22 Ds and 22 Ds reversed.
5. Cut 2 (2⅝" x 42") strips of sky blue fabric. From
these, cut 22 (2⅝") squares. Cut each square in half
diagonally to make 44 E triangles.
6. Cut 4 (6½" x 42") strips of sky blue fabric. From
these, cut 22 (4½" x 6½") Hs and 23 (1½" x 6½") Js.
7. Cut 2 (4½" x 42") strips of sky blue fabric. Cut these
into 1½"-wide segments to make 46 (1½" x 4½") Is.
8. Cut 5 (3¼" x 42") strips of sky blue fabric. From
these, cut 23 Ks and 23 Ks reversed.
9. Cut a 5½" x 42" strip of green fabric. Cut this into
1"-wide segments to make 22 (1" x 2½") F pieces and 23
(1" x 5½") Ls.

10. Cut 45 (3⅞") squares of green fabric. Cut each
square in half diagonally to make 90 G triangles.
11. From yellow print, cut 4 (5½" x 55") sashing strips.
Cut 2 (2½" x 65") strips and 2 (2½" x 81") strips for
inner border.
12. Cut 4 (4½" x 90") strips of floral fabric for outer borders and 4 (2½" x 90") strips for binding.

Traditional Piecing
1. Cut 7 (5¼") squares from each light solid fabric. Cut
squares in quarters diagonally to make 27 A triangles
(and 1 extra) of each color.
2. Join 2 As of the same color, matching short sides to
make a larger triangle. Make 9 triangle pairs of each
color. (It may seem strange to be joining pieces of the
same fabric, but the design of the tulip requires this
seam for visual balance.)
3. Sew blue Cs to 2 adjacent sides of each B. Press
seam allowances toward B.
4. Referring to Assembly diagrams, join an A of the
appropriate color to 1 side of each CBC unit. Press seam
allowances toward A. Join both halves of each tulip as
shown. Assemble 9 tulips of each color.

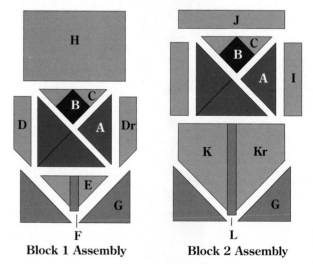

Block 1 Assembly   **Block 2 Assembly**

5. Aligning top edges, join an E to both sides of each F.
(Stem is slightly longer than triangles.) Join Ks and Ks
reversed to both sides of L stems in same manner.
Press seam allowances away from stems.
6. Follow Block Assembly diagrams to join remaining
pieces, making 22 of Block 1 and 23 of Block 2, distribut-
ing tulip colors evenly.

Our favorite spring
images include row
upon row of tulips
bowing gracefully
in the breeze. Turn
your bed into a field of
neatly planted rows with
multicolored tulips of
pastel patchwork.

Quick Piecing

This method shortens the marking, cutting, and sewing time for A triangle pairs. See page 148 for more detailed instructions on sewing quick-pieced triangles.

1. Cut 2 (9" x 13") strips of each light solid fabric for quick piecing. Cut remainder of each fabric into 3 (5¼") squares; then cut each square in quarters diagonally to get 11 (and 1 extra) A triangles of each fabric.

2. On wrong side of 1 (9" x 13") fabric piece of each color, draw 2 (5¼") squares as shown in Triangle-Square Grid. Draw diagonal lines through squares as shown.

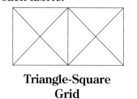

Triangle-Square Grid

3. Match each marked piece with its mate of the same color. Machine-sew grids, following directions for quarter-square triangles on page 149. Cut grids apart to make 8 triangle pairs from each grid. For the ninth tulip of each color, join 2 A triangles traditionally.

4. Follow steps 3–7 under Traditional Piecing to complete blocks.

Quilt Top Assembly

1. Referring to photo on page 31, arrange blocks in 5 horizontal rows of 9 blocks each. Alternate tall and short tulips in each row. Three rows have tall tulips (Block 2) at both ends, while 2 alternating rows begin and end with short tulips (Block 1). Distribute tulip colors as desired. When satisfied with arrangement, join blocks in each row.

2. Join yellow sashing strips between tulip rows. Press seam allowances toward sashing.

3. Add borders, mitering corners. See page 151 for tips on making mitered corners.

Quilting and Finishing

Quilt patchwork in-the-ditch. Quilt sashing and borders as desired. See page 157 for instructions on making and applying binding.

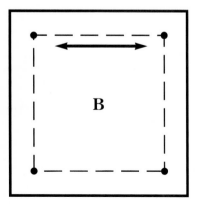

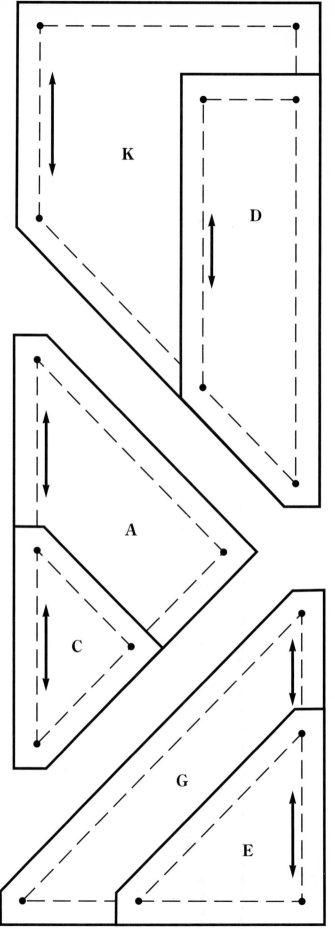

Dutch Treat Vest

Materials

Vest pattern (select any pattern with simple lines and a straight bottom, preferably without darts)

Blue chambray fabric for vest and lining fabric in amount required for pattern

¼ yard of grass-green fabric

5" squares of 5 dark solid fabrics for tulips

2" squares of 5 light solid fabrics for tulip centers

¾ yard each of tear-away stabilizer and paper-backed fusible web for machine appliqué

Graph paper and ruler

Appliqué Dutch Treat tulips onto a simple vest for a one-of-a-kind springtime garment.

Preparing for Machine Appliqué

Note: The following instructions are for machine appliqué as shown. To hand appliqué, add seam allowances to each piece and disregard references to fusible web and tear-away stabilizer.

1. Use pattern to cut vest pieces from chambray and lining fabric. On right side of each chambray piece, draw a light pencil line parallel to and 4¾" from bottom edge.

2. Set aside a 5¼" x 43" strip of green fabric for grass.

3. To make a pattern for the tulip shape, draw a 4" square on graph paper. Draw diagonal lines from corner to corner as shown in Diagram 1 and then erase top line of square.

Diagram 1

4. Trace tulip pattern 5 times on paper side of fusible web, leaving space between pieces. Draw 5 (1⅝") squares for tulip centers. For leaves, draw 5 (3") squares and draw 1 diagonal line through each square to make 10 triangles. For stems, draw 4 (½" x 3¼") strips and 1 (½" x 6½") strip. Cut shapes from web, including some excess around each drawn piece.

5. Following manufacturer's directions, fuse each piece of web to wrong side of appropriate fabric.

6. Cut appliqué pieces, following drawn lines. Remove paper backing.

7. Fuse 6½"-long stem in place at center back, positioning bottom edge of stem on drawn pencil line. Fuse a short stem in place on both sides of center stem, spacing them 3½" apart, as shown in Diagram 2.

8. Fuse a stem on each vest front, positioning it on the drawn line, 4" from center front edge.

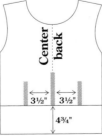

Diagram 2

9. Center a tulip atop each stem, with its bottom edge overlapping top ¼" of stem. (Make sure tulip sides stay out of vest seam allowances.) Tuck a coordinating tulip center under fabric in middle of each tulip. Fuse tulips in place.

10. Position and fuse leaves at bottom of center back stem, aligning bottom edges with drawn line. Fuse leaves for outer tulips, overlapping center leaves. Fuse leaves on front tulips.

11. Pin stabilizer to wrong side of vest under appliqués.

Appliqué and Finishing

1. Use matching thread and a medium-width satin stitch to appliqué leaves and stems. Do not stitch bottom edges, which will be covered by the green strip.

2. Appliqué tulips. Referring to photographs, extend 1 diagonal stitching line from center of tulip to opposite bottom corner. Remove stabilizer.

3. Position green strip on vest back with right sides facing, aligning bottom edge of strip with pencil line. Stitch, taking a ¼" seam allowance. Fold green fabric over to right side and trim strip to match side edges. Repeat with remaining green strip on fronts.

4. Baste raw edges of green fabric to vest fabric.

5. Join vest side seams. If desired, machine satin-stitch over horizontal seam line of green borders.

6. Complete vest following pattern directions.

*This field of flowers made
of bright, cheery scrap
fabrics from the 1930s
poses a challenge for the
quiltmaker with its
curved seams and set-ins.*

Garden of Friendship

Finished Size

Blocks: 59 full blocks, 8" square (plus 24 partial blocks)
Quilt: 77" x 100"

Materials

7½ yards of salmon-pink solid fabric
3 yards of green solid fabric
Scraps or ⅛ yard each of 8 light print fabrics for tulips
Scraps or ⅛ yard each of 8 dark print fabrics for flowerpots
Scraps or 11 "fat quarters" for prairie points
6 yards of backing fabric (or 3 yards of 90"-wide sheeting)

Cutting

1. See page 145 for tips on making templates. Make templates for patterns A–H.
2. From light print scraps, cut 77 As.
3. From dark print scraps, cut 77 Cs.
4. From green fabric, cut 2 (7½" x 82") and 2 (7½" x 58") strips for inner borders, and 4 (4") border squares.
5. From remaining green fabric, cut 75 Fs and 75 Fs reversed.
6. From pink fabric, cut 2 (4" x 72") and 2 (4" x 95") strips for outer borders.
7. From 26"-width of pink fabric leftover from borders, cut 77 Bs, 77 Ds, and 4 (7½") border squares.
8. Cut 21 (5" x 42") pink strips. From these, cut 70 Es, 70 Es reversed, 70 Gs, and 70 Gs reversed.
9. Cut 15 (4¼" x 42") pink strips. From these, cut 75 Hs and 75 Hs reversed.
10. Cut 130 (5") squares for prairie points.

Piecing

1. Join As and Bs, referring to page 148 for tips on stitching curved seams. (*Note:* The antique quilt shown has a seam in the center of the B piece. We eliminated that seam for ease of construction.)
2. Referring to Block Assembly diagram, sew an E and an E reversed piece to sides of a C flowerpot piece; then add a D triangle at bottom of unit.

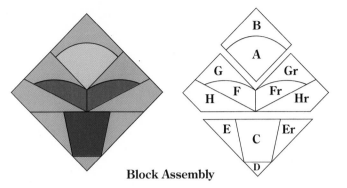

Block Assembly

3. Join F and G pieces. Sew an F reversed piece to a G reversed piece in the same manner. Add H and H reversed pieces to bottom of each unit.
4. Join an FGH unit to an FGH reversed unit.
5. Set an AB flower unit into FGH unit.
6. Complete block by sewing CDE unit to bottom of flower/leaf section. Repeat to make 59 blocks.
7. For right side of quilt, make 6 blocks without FGH reversed pieces (see Quilt Assembly diagram on page 36). For left side of quilt, make 6 more blocks, omitting FGH unit. Leave edges of these blocks uneven until after quilt top is assembled.
8. For top edge, make 6 partial blocks without A, B, G, and G reversed pieces. Since 2 of these partial blocks will be corners, you can also eliminate 1 side of leaf section on those 2 blocks as shown.
9. For bottom edge, assemble 6 partial blocks without CDE flowerpot units. Make 2 of these for corners, eliminating half of leaf section as shown.

Quilt Top Assembly

1. Follow Quilt Assembly diagram to join blocks in diagonal rows. Be sure to note type of partial block at ends of each row. Join rows.
2. Add a long green border strip to sides of quilt top, stitching over partial blocks as shown. Trim borders even with quilt top. Trim excess fabric of partial blocks even with seam allowance.
3. Stitch a pink square to 1 end of each remaining green border strip. Compare length of pieced border strip to top edge of quilt top and trim unstitched end as necessary, allowing for another square and seam allowance. Add pink square to trimmed end; then join border to

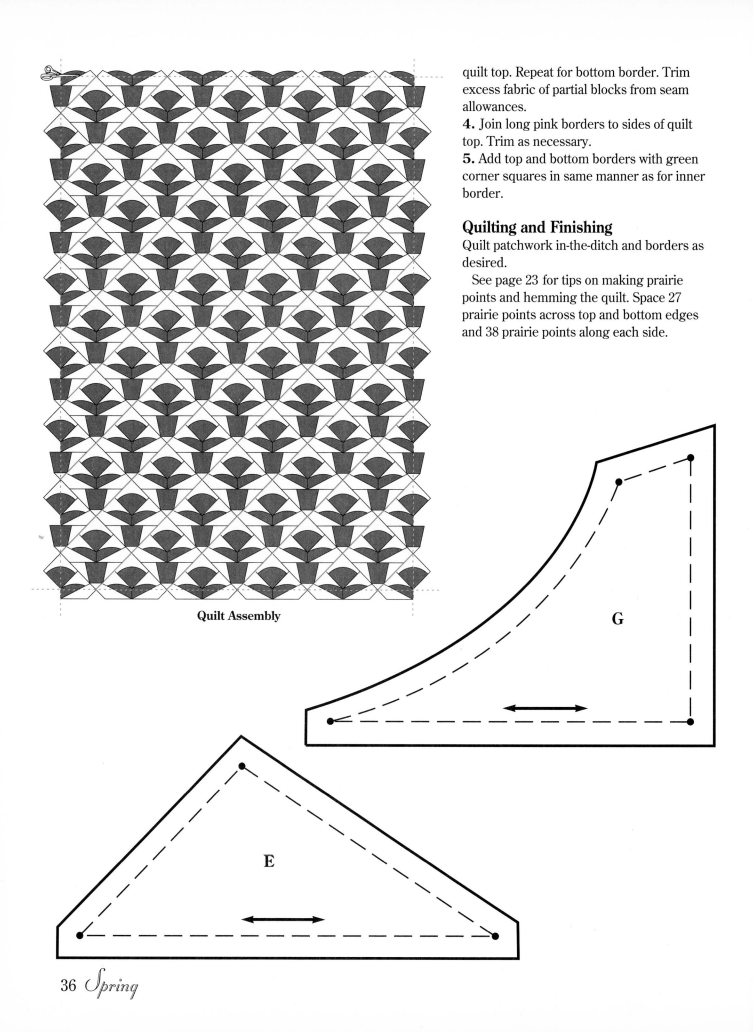

Quilt Assembly

quilt top. Repeat for bottom border. Trim excess fabric of partial blocks from seam allowances.

4. Join long pink borders to sides of quilt top. Trim as necessary.

5. Add top and bottom borders with green corner squares in same manner as for inner border.

Quilting and Finishing

Quilt patchwork in-the-ditch and borders as desired.

See page 23 for tips on making prairie points and hemming the quilt. Space 27 prairie points across top and bottom edges and 38 prairie points along each side.

G

E

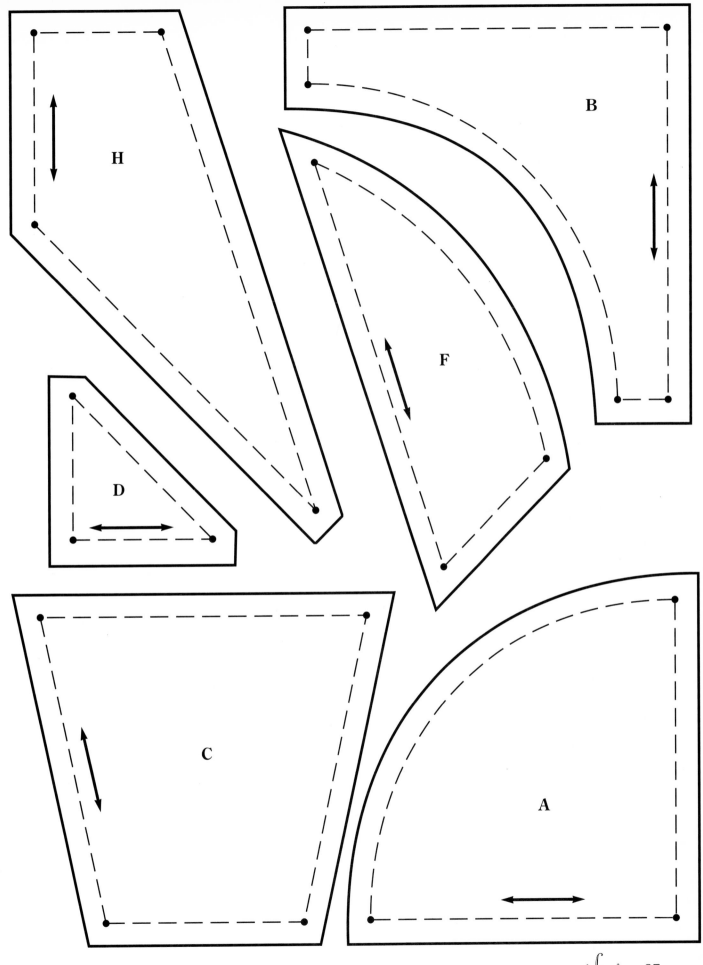

Iris in My Garden

Finished Size
Blocks: 20 blocks, 9½" square
Quilt: 71¾" x 85"

Materials
6 yards of muslin or white solid fabric
4 yards of green solid fabric (includes binding)
38 (3" x 6") scraps of assorted pastel solid fabrics for
   bottom flower petals (D)
38 (4"-square) scraps of assorted pastel solid fabrics for
   large flower petals (E)
5¼ yards of backing fabric
Embroidery floss to match flower fabrics and in
   assorted shades of gold or yellow for iris "beards"
Tracing paper and fabric marker

Cutting
1. From muslin, cut 8 (10" x 42") strips. Cut 4 (10")
squares from each strip.
2. Cut a 2½-yard length of muslin. From this, cut 2 (9½"
x 90") strips and 2 (9½" x 78") strips for borders.
3. For setting triangles, cut 2 (15" x 42") muslin strips.
From these, cut 4 (15") squares and 2 (7⅝") squares.
Cut large squares in quarters diagonally to make 14
(and 2 extra) X triangles. Cut small squares in half diagonally to make 4 Y corner triangles.
4. See page 145 for tips on making templates for
appliqué. Make a template for pieces A, B, C, D, and E
from pattern on page 40. For border leaves, make templates for F, G, and H on page 41.
5. Cut 2 (11" x 42") strips of green fabric. From 1 strip,
cut 10 each of A, B, and C with templates faceup, adding
seam allowances around each piece. From second strip,
cut 10 each of A, B, and C with templates facedown,
adding seam allowances.
6. Cut a 16" square of green fabric; then cut it into
1⅛"-wide *bias* strips. From these strips, cut 20 (5"-long)
stem pieces for iris blocks. From remaining strips, cut
18 (4¼"-long) stems for border irises.
7. Cut a 12" x 42" strip of green fabric. From this, cut 4
(10" x 12") rectangles. Fold each piece in half to measure 10" x 6", with wrong sides facing. Place F template
on fold as indicated on pattern. Cut 4 Fs.
8. From remaining green fabric, cut 4 Gs, 4 Gs
reversed, 14 Hs, and 14 Hs reversed.

9. Cut 38 E petals from 4" squares of assorted fabric
scraps. For each flower, choose a coordinating fabric
from which to cut 1 D and 1 D reversed. Lightly trace
embroidery details onto right side of each petal.

Appliqué and Embroidery
1. Make tracing of full-size iris pattern on page 40. On
back of paper, retrace drawing for reversed pattern.
2. Place a muslin square over tracing, aligning fabric
edges with corner placement lines at bottom of pattern.
Trace pattern onto fabric. Mark 10 blocks with tracing
faceup; trace 10 more blocks with pattern reversed.
3. Fold each stem strip in half lengthwise with wrong
sides facing. Stitch a scant ¼" from raw edge. Trim
seam allowances to ⅛". Press strip with seam at back.
4. Pin a stem on each block, aligning stem edges with
traced outline.
5. Turn under seam allowances of flower pieces, clipping as necessary. Do not turn under bottom edges of
leaves; these will be sewn into seam when blocks are
joined. Do not turn edges that will be covered by another piece, such as tops of D petals.
6. Position leaves on blocks. Appliqué stems and leaves.

Quilt Assembly

7. Position D petals and appliqué.

8. Using 2 strands of gold or yellow floss, work stem stitch "beards" on D petals. Then work running stitches around each beard.

9. Appliqué an E petal on each block.

10. Using 2 strands of matching floss, work stem stitch around center of each E petal and running-stitch detail at bottom of petals.

Quilt Top Assembly

Follow Quilt Assembly diagram to arrange appliquéd blocks, muslin squares, and setting triangles in diagonal rows. Join blocks in rows; then join rows.

Adding Appliqué Border

1. Mark centers on edges of border strips and quilt top. Matching centers, sew short strips to top and bottom edges. Add long strips to sides. Miter border corners.

2. Pin F leaves at corners. Following Quilt Assembly diagram, pin remaining leaves, stems, and irises in place. Each stem should be in line with tip of setting triangle directly above it and leaves cross at a point in line with tip of appliquéd block. Appliqué border pieces.

Quilting and Finishing

1. Lay the quilt on a flat surface for marking. First, mark outline quilting lines around all appliquéd irises.

2. See page 153 for tips on making a quilting stencil of iris pattern. Mark faceup iris design in plain blocks on right side of quilt. Turn stencil over to mark a reversed design in left-hand blocks. Alternate positions for center blocks. Add outline around each marked iris as for appliqués.
3. Measure and mark a diagonal grid across entire top, spacing lines ⅞" apart. Use block seams as guidelines for markings. Grid lines should not break through outline quilting.
4. Quilt on all marked lines. Our quilt also has veins of quilting through the center of every appliquéd leaf.
5. See page 157 for tips on making and applying binding.

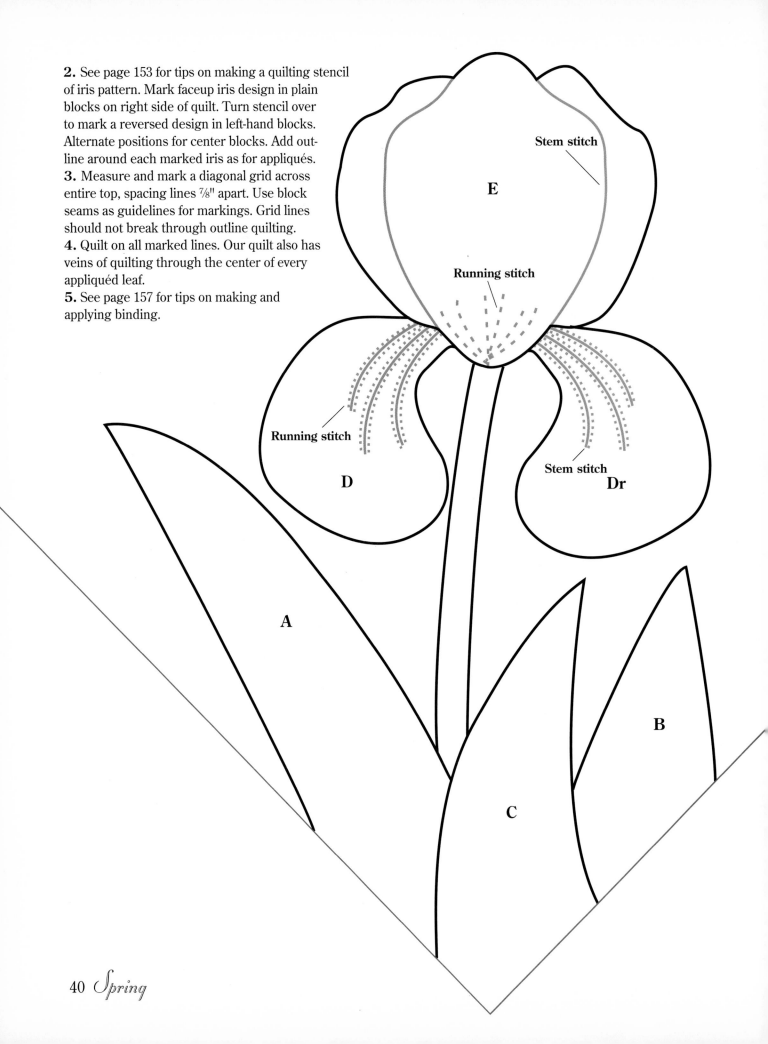

Stem stitch

E

Running stitch

Running stitch

D

Stem stitch

Dr

A

B

C

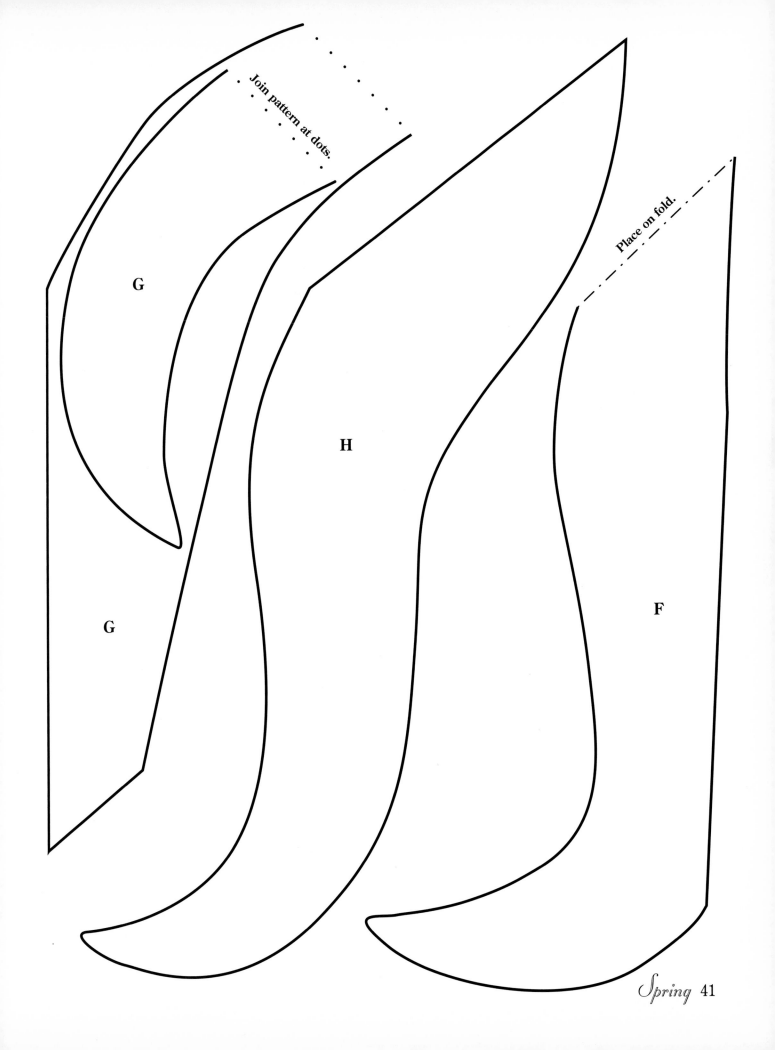

Join pattern at dots.

G

G

H

Place on fold.

F

Windblown Girl

Finished Size

Blocks: 30 appliquéd blocks, 9¼" square
Quilt: 78⅜" x 91½"

Materials

4½ yards of green solid fabric (includes binding)
2½ yards of muslin
⅛ yard of black solid fabric for shoes
30 (7" x 9") pieces of assorted print fabrics
30 (4") squares of coordinating solid fabrics
6 yards of backing fabric (or 2¾ yards of 90"-wide sheeting)
Assorted embroidery floss to match prints

Cutting

1. See page 145 for tips on making templates for appliqué. Make finished-size templates for dress/bonnet piece, sleeve, arm, pantaloons, and shoe.
2. Cut 8 (9¾" x 42") strips across width of muslin. From these strips, cut 30 (9¾") squares. Save leftover muslin for arms.
3. Cut 10 (9¾" x 42") strips across width of green fabric. From these, cut 38 (9¾") setting squares.
4. Set aside a 32" green square for binding.
5. From remaining green fabric, cut 4 (5" x 9¾") pieces and 22 (5")squares for border setting pieces.
6. Adding seam allowances, cut a dress/bonnet piece from each print fabric. Cut 15 of these with template faceup and 15 with template facedown. Keep right- and left-facing sets separate and match with other appliqué pieces as they are cut.

7. Cut 30 shoes from black fabric, cutting half with template facedown.
8. From each coordinating solid fabric, cut 1 sleeve and 1 pantaloons, cutting 15 sets with templates facedown.
9. Clip seam allowances of appliqué pieces at curves and points. Turn under seam allowances. Do not turn under edges that will be covered by another piece, such as top edges of arms, pantaloons, and shoes.

Appliqué and Embroidery

1. Fold each muslin square in half vertically, horizontally, and diagonally, finger-pressing folds to establish placement guidelines.
2. Position each square over dress/bonnet pattern on page 45, matching centers and aligning creased placement lines with centering guideline on pattern. Lightly trace pattern and bonnet tie embroidery lines on each block.
3. Pin a dress/bonnet piece in place on each block, aligning edges with traced outline. Pin pantaloons and shoes in place. Appliqué, working from bottom to top.
4. Position arm and sleeve on each dress and appliqué.
5. Using 2 strands of contrasting floss, work small lazy daisy stitches on pantaloons and buttonhole stitches at bottom edges of sleeve and pantaloons. Work bonnet ties in outline stitch and hatband in running stitch, using same floss or a different color.

Quilt Top Assembly

1. Refer to Quilt Assembly diagram to arrange 30 appliquéd blocks and 38 green setting squares in diagonal rows. Note that all girls face same direction in each diagonal row. Join blocks in rows. Press seam allowances toward setting squares.

Quilt Assembly

While away breezy days of spring with appliqué, making calico scraps into wind-tossed girls. Set with squares of a favorite color, the quilt's irregular edge makes an interesting finish.

not trim batting and backing to match jagged edge of top until quilting is complete. Outline-quilt around each girl and on all marked lines. When quilting is complete, trim batting and backing even with quilt top.

See page 157 for instructions on making and applying binding.

2. Following diagram, add 5" green squares to row ends. Note that center 2 rows do not have small squares attached and both adjacent rows have small squares at 1 end only.

3. Join diagonal rows.

4. Join remaining 5" squares to ends of each 5" x 9¾" piece. Press seam allowances toward center. Following diagram, join a pieced unit at corners of quilt top.

Quilting and Finishing

See page 153 for tips on making stencils of full-size quilting designs. Referring to photograph, mark feathered wreath design on 20 interior setting blocks. Mark hearts design on small border squares.

Mark lines of diagonal cross-hatching on each appliquéd block, spacing them approximately 1⅛" apart. Extend lines into outer setting squares.

Sandwich batting between quilt top and backing fabric. Baste layers together. Do

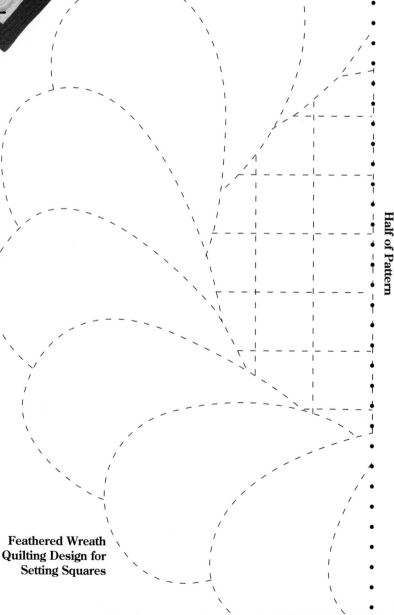

Half of Pattern

**Feathered Wreath
Quilting Design for
Setting Squares**

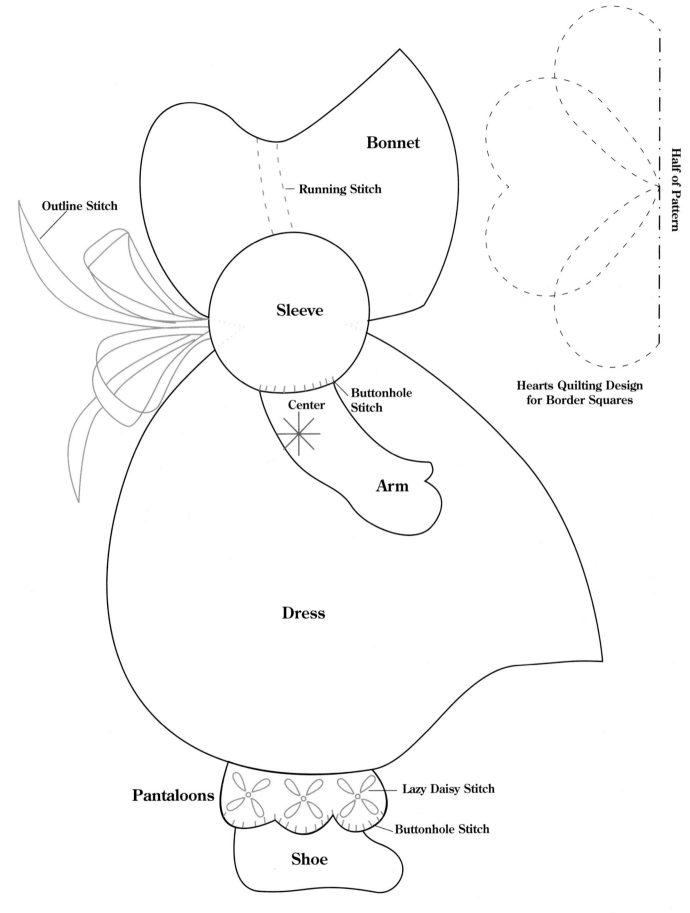

Bonnet

— Running Stitch

Outline Stitch

Sleeve

Buttonhole
Stitch

Center

Arm

Dress

Pantaloons — Lazy Daisy Stitch

— Buttonhole Stitch

Shoe

Half of Pattern

**Hearts Quilting Design
for Border Squares**

Spring 45

Summer

Summer's put the idea in
 My head that I'm a boy agin;
And all around's so bright and gay
 I want to put my team away,
And jest git out whare I can lay
 And soak my hide full of the day!

James Whitcomb Riley, "A Summer's Day"

Celebrations fill the hot, lazy days of summer with weddings, reunions, fireworks, and family vacations. When the easy living of swimming, barbecues, and sipping lemonade on the porch gives way to chill winds, these quilts bring back memories of nature's heyday and summer's warm, gentle nights.

Wedding Ring

Finished Size
Blocks: 20 blocks, 11¼" square
Quilt: 67" x 83¾"

Materials
4¾ yards of white solid fabric
2¾ yards of blue print fabric (includes binding)
5 yards of backing fabric

Cutting
Note: Cutting instructions for patchwork pieces differ for traditional piecing and quick piecing. The following instructions are for the white setting pieces only, which are cut the same way for both methods. Cutting instructions for patchwork pieces are given with directions for each technique.

1. Cut 4 (11¾" x 42") strips of white fabric. From these, cut 12 (11¾") setting squares.

2. Cut 4 (17¼") white squares. Cut these in quarters diagonally to make 14 (and 2 extra) X setting triangles.

3. Cut 2 (9") white squares. Cut these in half diagonally to make 4 Y corner triangles.

Traditional Piecing
1. See page 145 for tips on making templates. Make templates for patterns A and B.

2. From white fabric, cut 320 As and 100 Bs.

3. From blue fabric, cut 320 As and 80 Bs.

4. Join blue and white Bs in pairs, leaving 20 white Bs leftover. Press seam allowances toward blue fabric.

5. Join blue and white As, making triangle-squares. Press all seam allowances toward blue fabric.

6. Join triangle-squares in pairs; then combine pairs to make a 4-square unit as shown in Block Assembly diagram. Make 4 pieced units for each block.

7. Following Block Assembly diagram, join pieced units in horizontal rows. For all top and bottom rows, press joining seam allowances toward center squares. For middle rows, press joining seam allowances away from center. Join rows. Make 20 blocks.

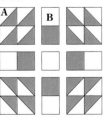

Block Assembly

Quick Piecing
The Wedding Ring block is ideal for quick piecing shortcuts. All the triangle-squares and square pairs can be quick-pieced. See page 148 for more instructions on quick-pieced triangle-squares.

1. Cut 6 (2¾" x 42") crossgrain strips of each fabric.

2. Join each blue strip to a white strip along 1 long edge. Press all seam allowances toward blue fabric. Cut 14 (2¾"-wide) segments from each strip set.

3. Cut 2 more 2¾" x 42" strips from white fabric. From these, cut 20 (2¾") squares.

4. Cut 10 (14") squares of each fabric. On wrong side of each white square, mark a 4 x 4-square grid of 3⅛" squares. Draw a diagonal line through each square as shown in Triangle-Square Grid diagram.

Triangle-Square Grid

5. Pin white squares to blue squares, with right sides facing. Following directions for half-square triangles on page 149, machine-stitch grids. Cut 32 triangle-squares from each grid.

Quilt Assembly

6. Follow steps 6 and 7 under Traditional Piecing to make 20 Wedding Ring blocks.

Quilt Top Assembly

Referring to Quilt Assembly diagram, arrange blocks in diagonal rows with setting squares between blocks. Join blocks and squares in each row. Add setting and corner triangles to row ends. Press seam allowances toward setting pieces. Join rows to assemble quilt top.

Quilting and Finishing

Outline-quilt patchwork. Quilt setting squares, sashing, and borders as desired. See page 157 for instructions on making and applying binding.

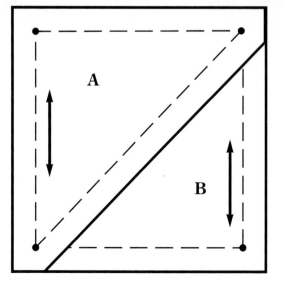

Sailboat Crib Quilt

Finished Size

Blocks: 12 blocks, 10" square
Quilt: 40" x 52½"

Materials

2¼ yards of white solid fabric
9" x 22" pieces of 6 assorted blue print and green
    print fabrics
⅜ yard of binding fabric
1⅝ yards of backing fabric

Cutting

Note: Cutting instructions for patchwork differ for traditional and quick piecing. The following instructions are for borders and sashing, which are cut the same way for both methods. Directions for cutting patchwork pieces are given with instructions for each technique.

1. Cut 2 (3" x 54") white strips for side borders.
2. Set aside a ½-yard length of white fabric for A squares and a 16" x 54" piece for B triangles.
3. From remaining white fabric, cut 5 (3" x 36") strips and 8 (3" x 11") strips for sashing.

Traditional Piecing

1. See page 145 for tips on making templates. Make templates for patterns A and B.
2. Cut a 6" square of each print fabric. From each square, cut 4 As.
3. Cut 16 Bs from each print fabric.
4. From white fabric, cut 72 As and 96 Bs.
5. Join each print B to a white B to make a triangle-square. Press all seam allowances toward blue fabrics.

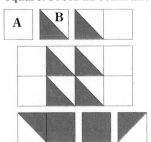

Block Assembly

6. Follow Block Assembly diagram to join As and pieced B triangle-squares to make 4 horizontal rows for each block. Join rows. Make 6 blocks as shown in diagram. Make 6 more blocks that sail in opposite direction by turning triangle-squares appropriately.

Quick Piecing

1. Cut a 6" square of each print fabric. From each square, cut 4 (3") squares (As).
2. Cut ½-yard piece of white fabric into 6 (3" x 42") strips. From these, cut 72 (3") squares (As).
3. Cut a 9" x 16" piece of each print fabric. Cut 6 matching pieces from 16" x 54" white fabric piece.
4. On wrong side of each white rectangle, draw a 2 x 4-square grid of 3⅜" squares. Draw diagonal lines through squares as shown in Triangle-Square Grid diagram.

Triangle-Square Grid

5. Layer print and white fabrics with right sides facing and with marked grid faceup. Pin fabrics together at corners and centers, avoiding diagonal lines.
6. See page 148 for more details on sewing quick-pieced triangles. Following directions for half-square triangles, machine-stitch grids. Cut grids apart to make 16 triangle-squares from each grid.
7. Follow Step 6 under Traditional Piecing to make 12 blocks.

Quilt Top Assembly

1. Referring to photograph, arrange blocks in 4 horizontal rows of 3 blocks each with an 11" vertical sashing strip between blocks. All blocks in each row sail in the

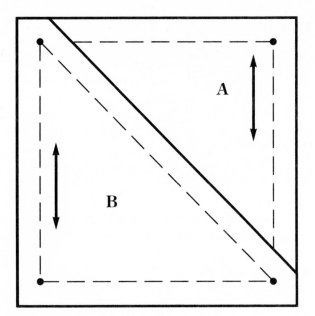

Quick piecing techniques can make sailing on fabric waters a year-round memory of summer's warm and gentle breezes in this endearing little quilt, perfect for a wall hanging or child's quilt.

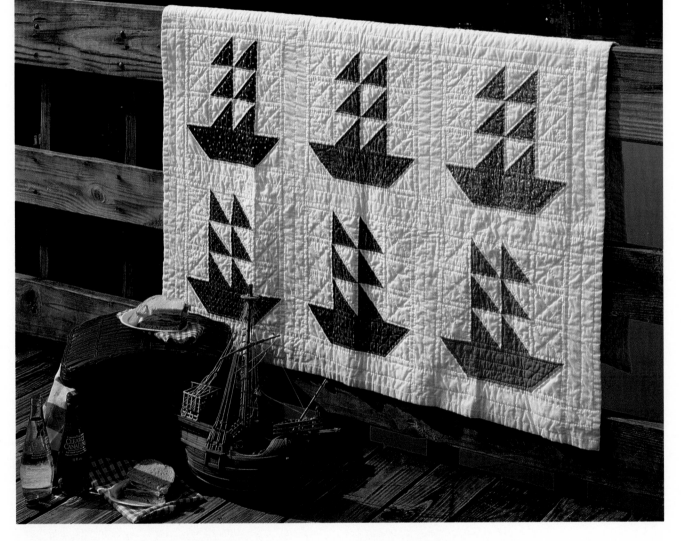

same direction. Join blocks and sashing in each row. Press seam allowances toward sashing.

2. Join a 36" horizontal sashing strip to top edge of each row. Press seam allowances toward sashing.

3. Join rows, alternating direction of blocks as shown. Add remaining sashing strip at bottom of Row 4.

4. Join side borders to quilt top.

Quilting and Finishing

Outline-quilt patchwork, adding an "X" of quilting in each white A square. If desired, add additional quilting at the bottom of each boat to represent water lines. Quilt sashing and borders as desired.

See page 157 for instructions on making and applying binding.

Say hooray for the U.S.A. with a patchwork sea of stars. This quilt's patriotic colors will keep Independence Day picnics and late-night fireworks warm in your heart every day of the year.

Seven Sisters

Finished Size
Blocks: 20 blocks, 13⅛" x 15"
Quilt: 70" x 87⅝"

Materials
4 yards each of muslin and blue print fabric
2⅝ yards of red print fabric (includes binding)
5⅜ yards of backing fabric

Cutting
1. See page 145 for tips on making templates. Make templates for patterns A, B, C, and D.
2. From blue, cut 840 As.
3. Cut 30 (2⅞" x 42") strips of muslin. From these, cut 360 As and 120 Bs.
4. Cut 30 Cs, 10 Ds, and 10 Ds reversed from remaining muslin.
5. For red borders, cut 2 (5½" x 94") and 2 (5½" x 76") strips.
6. Cut 4 (3½" x 61") strips of red fabric for sashing.

Piecing
Join 6 blue As to form a star, referring to Star Piecing diagram. Make 7 stars for each block. Referring to Block Assembly diagram, join 7 stars with 18 muslin As and 6 muslin Bs. See page 148 for tips on sewing set-in seams. Make 20 blocks.

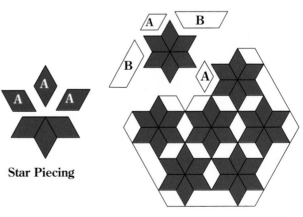

Star Piecing

Block Assembly

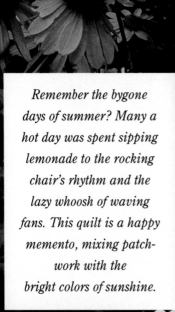

Paper Fans

Finished Size
Blocks: 30 blocks, 12" square
Quilt: 60" x 72"

Materials
3 yards of muslin
¾ yard of blue solid fabric
240 (3" x 10") scraps of assorted print fabrics
⅝ yard of binding fabric
4¾ yards of backing fabric

Cutting
1. See page 145 for tips on making templates. Make templates for patterns A, B, and C.
2. From scraps, cut 240 As.
3. Cut 30 Bs from blue fabric and 30 Cs from muslin.

Piecing
1. Following Block Assembly diagram, join 8 As for each fan. Press seam allowances to 1 side.
2. Join a B piece to the bottom of each fan. (See page 148 for tips on stitching curved seams.) Press seam allowances toward Bs.
3. Set each fan into a muslin C piece to complete 30 blocks.

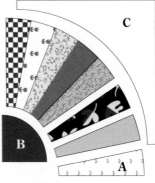

Block Assembly

Quilt Top Assembly
Referring to photograph on page 58, join blocks in 6 horizontal rows of 5 blocks each. Join rows.

Quilting and Finishing
Make a stencil for quilting design printed inside Pattern C. Quilt this motif in muslin areas of each block. Outline-quilt patchwork.

See page 157 for tips on making and applying binding.

Remember the bygone days of summer? Many a hot day was spent sipping lemonade to the rocking chair's rhythm and the lazy whoosh of waving fans. This quilt is a happy memento, mixing patchwork with the bright colors of sunshine.

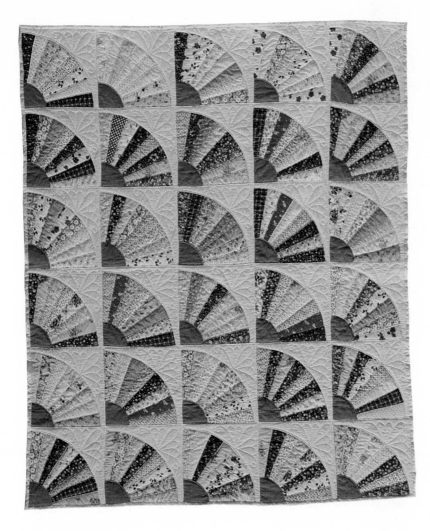

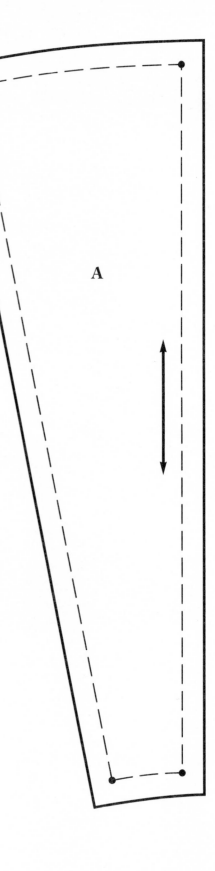

A

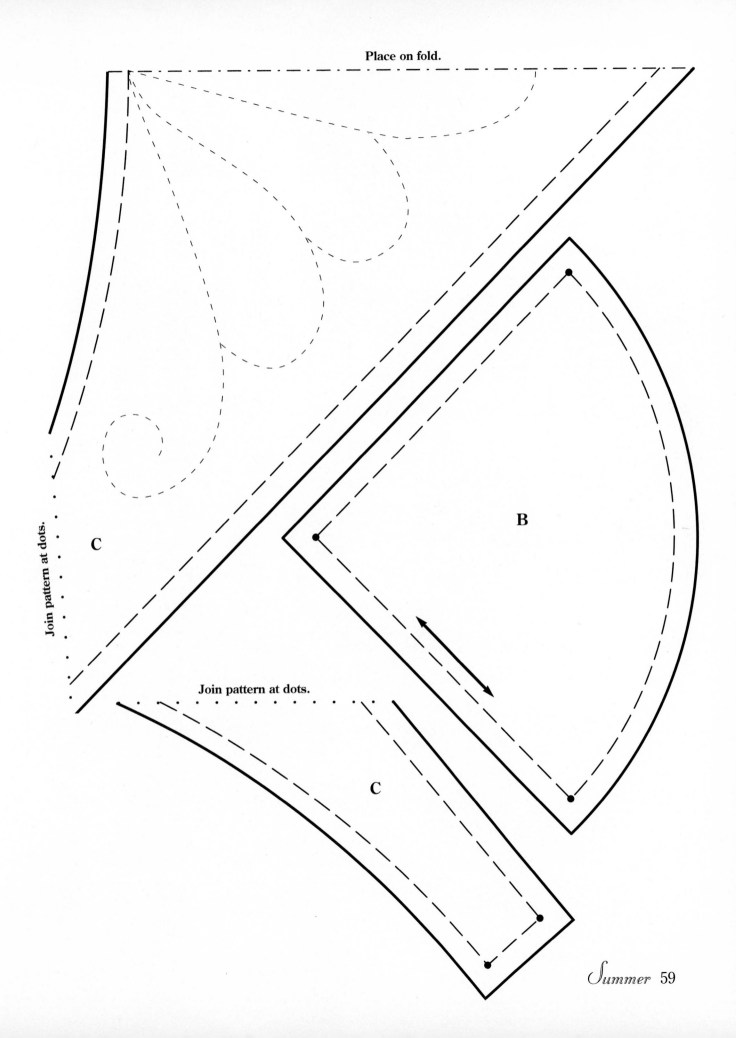

Place on fold.

Join pattern at dots.

C

B

Join pattern at dots.

C

A rose is the most elegant of summer flowers, extravagantly fragrant and colorful. Use fabrics that reflect the colors of your favorite rose in this patchwork version of a formal garden.

Rose Garden

Finished Size
Blocks: 30 blocks, 15" square
Quilt: 84" x 99"

Materials
4½ yards of rose print fabric (includes binding)
3 yards of cream print fabric
2⅝ yards of cream solid fabric
7¾ yards of backing fabric (or 3 yards of 90"-wide
   sheeting)

Cutting
1. For borders, cut 4 (3½" x 95") strips of rose print fabric and 4 (2" x 92") strips of cream solid fabric. Set aside ¾ yard of rose print fabric for binding.
2. See page 145 for tips on making templates. Make templates for patterns A–E.
3. From cream print fabric, cut 150 As, 240 Bs, and 120 Ds.
4. From cream solid fabric, cut 120 Es.
5. From 27" x 43" of rose print fabric, cut 240 Bs.
6. From remaining rose print fabric, cut 120 Cs.

Piecing
1. Referring to Block Assembly diagram, join all B triangles in pairs of contrasting colors as shown. Press seam allowances toward darker fabric.
2. Join C and D pieces as shown. Press seam allowances toward C pieces.
3. Join an A square, pieced B triangles, and a

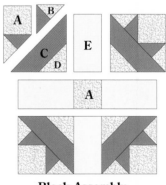

Block Assembly

CD unit as shown in diagram to make a corner section. Make 4 corners for each block.
4. Join corner units and E strips into horizontal rows for each block as shown. Press seam allowances toward Es.

Gone Fishin'

Finished Size
Blocks: 12 blocks, 16½" square
Quilt: 65" x 81"

Materials
3½ yards of white fabric
1⅞ yards of striped fabric (includes binding)
1½ yards each of turquoise solid and tropical
print fabric
5 yards of backing fabric

Cutting
1. See page 145 for tips on making templates. Make templates for patterns A–H.
2. From both turquoise solid and print fabrics, cut 64 As and 128 Bs. Set aside 16 As and 32 Bs of each color for outer border.
3. Cut 19 (2¾" x 42") strips of white fabric. From these, cut 96 Cs, 32 Hs, and 32 Hs reversed.
4. Cut 19 (2¼" x 42") white strips. From these, cut 96 Ds, 32 Fs, 32 Gs, and 32 Gs reversed.
5. From remaining white fabric, cut 48 Es.
6. For borders, cut 2 (4" x 67") strips, 2 (3¾" x 58") strips, and 4 (4¾") squares of striped fabric. Cut and set aside a 24" square of striped fabric for bias binding.

Piecing
1. Referring to Block Assembly diagram, join solid and print A diamonds in pairs. Press all seam allowances toward solid diamonds. Make 4 pairs for each block.

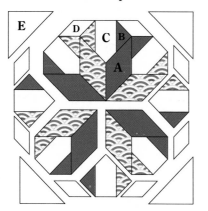

Block Assembly

2. Join B triangles to opposite sides of each C piece as follows. Referring to Block Assembly diagram, make 4 units with print triangles on the right and a solid triangle on the left; for remaining 4 units, reverse color placement. Press seam allowances toward B triangles. Make 8 BCB units for each block.
3. Set a BCB unit into the opening of each diamond pair, matching colors of As and Bs. See page 148 for tips on sewing set-in seams.
4. Join diamond pairs as shown in Block Assembly diagram; then set a BCB unit into each new opening as shown.
5. Set in D diamonds around each block. Finish each block with an E triangle at each corner. Make 12 blocks.

Quilt Top Assembly
Referring to Quilt Assembly diagram, join blocks in 4 horizontal rows of 3 blocks each. Join rows.

Add 4"-wide borders to side edges; then join remaining borders to top and bottom. (*Note:* The ¼" difference in border widths is necessary to accommodate piecing of outer border.)

Piecing Outer Border
Referring to Border Block Assembly diagram, piece 16 print fish and 16 turquoise solid fish, using remaining As and Bs.

Border Block Assembly

Referring to Quilt Assembly diagram on page 66, join 9 fish, alternating colors, for each side border. Join side borders to quilt as shown.

Join 7 blocks as shown for top border, adding a striped square at both ends. Add border to top edge of quilt. Repeat for bottom border.

Quilting and Finishing
Outline-quilt patchwork. Use remaining 24" square of striped fabric to make bias binding. See page 157 for instructions on making and applying binding.

Use your wildest,
brightest fabrics to make
an ocean of tropical fish
aswim in clear waters.
Piece blocks that blend
hot prints with cool white
to keep summer's colors
vivid long after
vacation is over.

Go off to the beach with an easy-to-make appliquéd tote. Big enough for a family's towels and toys, it's an eye-catching accessory that's practical, too.

Gone Fishin' Beach Bag

Finished Size: 21½" x 22"

Materials

⅔ yard each of canvaslike white woven fabric and striped cotton fabric
⅓ yard each of tropical print and turquoise solid fabrics
⅔ yard each of paper-backed fusible web and tear-away stabilizer for machine appliqué
1½ yards of 1"-wide nylon belting
Liquid ravel preventer

Preparing for Machine Appliqué

Note: The following instructions are for machine appliqué as shown. To hand appliqué, use A and B patterns (with seam allowances) to cut pieces and disregard references to fusible web and tear-away stabilizer.

1. From white fabric, cut a 24" x 44" rectangle. Cut a matching piece from striped fabric for lining. Cut and set aside 2 (1½" x 28") strips of print fabric for handles.
2. To mark handle placement, place a pin or chalk mark 8" from each corner on each end on right side of white fabric (see Diagram 1).

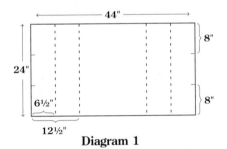

Diagram 1

3. Lightly draw a line 12½" from each end, as shown in Diagram 1. Draw 2 more lines, this time measuring 6½" from each end.
4. Trace 12 As on paper side of fusible web, drawing on sewing line only (finished size) and leaving a little space between pieces. To add tail, trace 2 Bs on each A in the same manner to complete each fish. Cut each fish from web, adding a little extra around each shape.
5. Following manufacturer's directions, fuse 6 fish each to wrong sides of print and solid appliqué fabrics.
6. Cut out appliqué pieces, following traced lines on webbing. Remove paper backing.
7. With right sides up and short side of rectangle at the top, center 3 turquoise fish on 6½" line, with each fish's nose on drawn line and pointing right. Keep fish out of ½"-wide seam allowances at sides. Fuse fish in place. Turn fabric around and repeat, fusing remaining 3 turquoise fish on opposite 6½" line.

8. Fuse print fish on 12½" lines in the same manner, pointing them left.
9. Pin stabilizer to wrong side of white fabric under appliqués.

Machine Appliqué

Use turquoise thread and a medium-width satin stitch to appliqué fish as shown in Diagram 2, pivoting fabric to change directions without lifting needle. Tear stabilizer away from stitching when appliqué is complete.

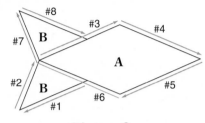

Diagram 2

Finishing Beach Bag

1. With right sides facing and short ends aligned, fold white rectangle in half. Stitch side seams with ½" seam allowances.
2. Press side seams open; then press under a ⅝"-deep hem around top edge. Lightly press fold line at bottom of bag. Do not turn bag.
3. To make squared bottom, align pressed bottom fold line with 1 side seam to form a triangle as shown in Diagram 3. Pin bottom and side seams together 3" from tip of triangle.

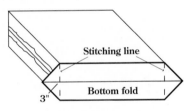

Diagram 3

Flatten bottom and stitch across base of triangle. Repeat for opposite corner. Trim triangles ½" from seam line. Turn bag right side out.
4. Repeat steps 1–3 to prepare lining fabric.
5. Cut 2 (27") lengths of belting. Apply liquid ravel preventer to raw edges.
6. Press a scant ½" hem on both long edges of 1½"-wide strips of print fabric, making each folded strip ½" to ⅝" wide.
7. Center a pressed strip, right side up, on each belting piece. Topstitch edges.
8. With right sides facing and edges aligned, center ends of 1 belting piece over placement marks on 1 top edge of tote. Baste in place. Repeat on opposite edge.
9. Insert lining into tote, with wrong sides facing. Match side seams and pressed top edges. Topstitch ⅛" from top edge through both layers. Sew another line of topstitching ¼" below first line.

*If summer's barefoot boy
comes home with pockets
full of snips and snails,
satisfy his craving
for indoor amphibians
with this original design.
This small quilt is comfy
and cozy for
napping children.*

Turtle Creek

Finished Size
Block: 12 blocks, 12" square
Quilt: 48" x 63"

Materials
1⅜ yards of blue print fabric
1¼ yards each of blue solid fabric and dark green print fabric
¾ yard of yellow print fabric (includes binding)
⅝ yard of light green print or striped fabric
½ yard of brown solid fabric
3 yards of backing fabric
1 skein of yellow embroidery floss

Cutting
1. See page 145 for tips on making templates. Make templates of patterns A, B, D, E, F, and H. Mark horizontal placement lines on Template F.
2. From brown fabric, cut 12 As, 12 Ds, and 48 Es.
3. Cut 6 (2½" x 42") strips of yellow print for binding. From remaining yellow print fabric, cut 20 (3½") sashing squares.
4. Cut 7 (1⅞" x 43") strips of light green fabric.
5. From dark green fabric, cut 14 (2⅜" x 43") strips.
6. From solid blue fabric, cut 2 (5¼" x 42") strips. From these, cut 24 (2½" x 5¼") C pieces.
7. Cut 6 (2" x 42") blue strips. From these, cut 24 (2" x 9½") G pieces.
8. From remaining solid blue fabric, cut 24 Bs, 96 Ds, 12 Hs, and 12 Hs reversed.
9. Cut blue print fabric into 11 (3½" x 42") strips. From these, cut 31 (3½" x 12½") sashing strips.

Piecing
Section 1: Join a blue B to each diagonal edge of an A. Press seam allowances toward A. Referring to Block Assembly diagram, join a C to both sides of AB unit. Press seam allowances toward Cs.
Section 2: Join a dark green strip to both sides of each light green strip. Press seam allowances toward bottom of each pieced strip.
  Position Template F on 1 strip, aligning placement lines on template with seam lines. (The template's top point should meet 1 edge of the strip, and bottom of

template will be approximately ¾" from opposite edge.) Mark and cut 1 F.
  Referring to Cutting diagram, rotate template so its point is at opposite fabric edge, aligning placement lines and diagonal edges of template and fabric. Continue cutting pieces as shown to make 48 Fs.

Cutting

  Join a blue D triangle to both straight sides of an E. Press seam allowances toward E. Make 48 DE units.
  Sew bottom of each F unit to diagonal edge of a DE unit, making a square. Press seam allowances toward F.
  Join 2 DEF squares, selecting pairs with opposing seam allowances. Press center seam allowances to 1 side. Join 2 pair to make 12 units.
  Add G strips to both sides of DEF unit to complete section.
Section 3: Sew a brown D triangle between an H and an H reversed piece, as shown in Block Assembly diagram. Press seam allowances toward H pieces.
Assembly: Join sections 1, 2, and 3 as shown in Block Assembly diagram. Make 12 turtle blocks.
  Use 3 strands of embroidery floss to make French knots for turtles' eyes.

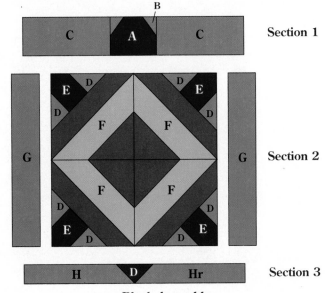

Block Assembly

Quilt Top Assembly

1. Follow Quilt Assembly diagram to arrange blocks in 4 horizontal rows of 3 blocks each. Join rows with sashing strips between blocks. Add sashing strips to ends of rows. Press seam allowances toward sashing.

2. Make 5 rows of horizontal sashing, joining 4 yellow squares and 3 sashing strips in each row. Press seam allowances toward sashing.

3. Join rows, alternating sashing rows and block rows as shown.

Quilting and Finishing

Outline-quilt patchwork. Quilt sashing as desired. See page 157 for instructions on making and applying straight-grain binding.

Quilt Assembly

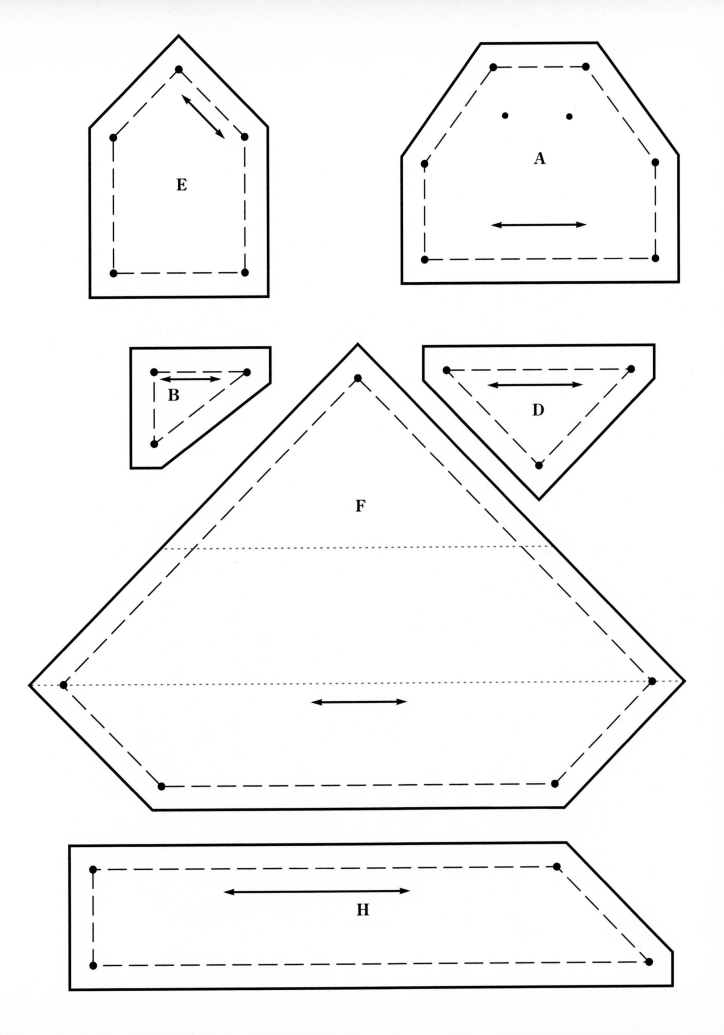

Autumn

October gave a party;
　　The leaves by hundreds came—
The Chestnuts, Oaks, and Maples,
　　And leaves of every name.
The Sunshine spread a carpet,
　　And everything was grand,
Miss Weather led the dancing,
　　Professor Wind the band.
The Chestnuts came in yellow,
　　The Oaks in crimson dressed;
The lovely Misses Maple
　　In scarlet looked their best;
All balanced to their partners,
　　And gaily fluttered by;
The sight was like a rainbow
　　New fallen from the sky.
Then, in the rustic hollow,
　　At hide-and-seek they played,
The party closed at sundown,
　　But everybody stayed.

George Cooper, "October's Party"

Leaves are the templates of autumn's quilts,
dressed in the season's brilliant wardrobe of
gold, green, copper, scarlet, and richest brown.
When the frost gleams on the pumpkin, these
quilts retain the warmth of Indian Summer,
bountiful harvests, and prayers of Thanksgiving.

Indian Summer

Finished Size
Blocks: 72 blocks, 8" square
Quilt: 77½" x 87"

Materials
4½ yards of muslin (includes binding)
2 yards of brown plaid fabric
⅜ yard of brown solid fabric
Scraps or 12 (¼-yard) pieces of assorted gold, dark green, tan, rust, and brown print fabrics
5¼ yards of backing fabric (or 2⅝ yards of 90"-wide sheeting)
2 skeins of black embroidery floss

Cutting
1. See page 145 for tips on making templates for appliqué. Make a finished-size template for leaf pattern on page 78, or use real leaves as patterns.
2. Trace leaf template on right side of print fabrics, marking embroidery details on each leaf. Adding seam allowances, cut 72 leaves.
3. Cut 15 (8½" x 42½") strips of muslin. From these, cut 72 (8½") squares.
4. Cut 8 (8½" x 42") strips of plaid fabric. Cut 2"-wide segments from each strip to make 161 (2" x 8½") sashing pieces.
5. Cut 5 (2" x 42") strips of brown fabric. From these, cut 90 (2") squares for sashing.

Appliqué
1. Fold each muslin square in half vertically, horizontally, and diagonally, finger-pressing folds to establish placement guidelines.
2. Position each square over leaf pattern on page 78, matching center of fabric with marked center on pattern. Lightly trace leaf and stem outlines on muslin.
3. Turn under seam allowances on leaf pieces. Pin in place on muslin, aligning edges with traced outlines. Appliqué 72 leaf blocks.
4. Using 2 strands of floss, work leaf veins and stems in outline stitch.

A favorite image of autumn's balmy days is a shower of glowing leaves, fluttering on a breeze. Use vivid earth-tone fabrics to appliqué these dancing leaves within a framework of simple sashing.

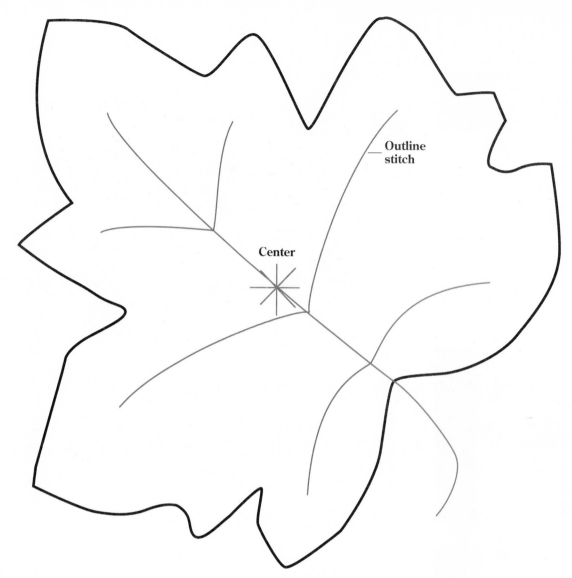

Outline stitch

Center

Quilt Top Assembly

1. Refer to photograph and Row Assembly diagram to arrange blocks in 9 horizontal rows of 8 blocks each. Turn blocks to position leaves as desired.

2. Join blocks in each row with sashing strips between blocks and at row ends as shown. Press seam allowances toward sashing strips.

3. Referring to Row Assembly diagram, piece 10 rows of sashing strips and sashing squares. Press seam allowances toward strips.

4. Join rows, alternating sashing rows and block rows.

Quilting and Finishing

Outline-quilt leaves and sashing squares. Use remaining muslin to make straight-grain binding. See page 157 for instructions on making and applying binding.

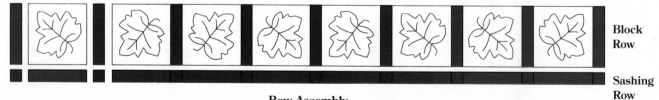

Block Row

Sashing Row

Row Assembly

Wild Goose Chase Lap Quilt

The honking cry of
migrating geese is a sure
sign of changing seasons.
The triangle patchwork
of this traditional
pattern, reminiscent of
those flying formations,
uses up a multitude of
fabric scraps.

Wild Goose Chase Lap Quilt

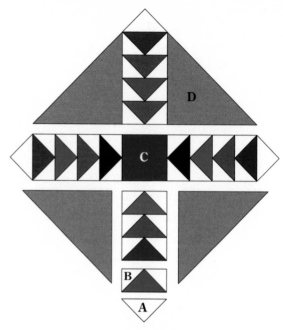

Block Assembly

Finished Size
Blocks: 16 blocks, 12¾" square
Quilt: 56" x 56"

Materials
1¾ yards of muslin (includes binding)
1⅝ yards of brown solid fabric for inner border
1⅝ yards of 3½"-wide border print or striped fabric
  for outer border
1⅛ yards of tan print fabric
Scraps or 11 (⅛-yard) pieces of assorted print fabrics
3⅜ yards of backing fabric

Cutting
1. See page 145 for tips on making templates. Make templates for patterns A–D.
2. Cut 1 or 2 Cs from each scrap fabric to make 16 Cs. From remaining print fabric, cut 256 As.
3. Set aside a 24" square of muslin for bias binding or 6 (2½" x 42") strips for straight-grain binding. From remaining muslin, cut 64 As and 512 Bs.
4. Cut 16 (9¾") squares from tan print fabric. Cut 4 Ds from each square by cutting each square in quarters diagonally.
5. For borders, cut 4 (1½" x 57") strips of brown solid fabric and 4 (4" x 57") strips of border print.

Piecing
1. To make Wild Goose units, join a muslin B to both short legs of each print A as shown in Piecing diagram. Press seam allowance toward Bs.

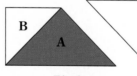

Piecing

2. Referring to Block Assembly diagram, join pieced units in groups of 4. Add a muslin A to bottom of each Wild Goose strip as shown.

3. For each block, join Ds to long sides of 2 Wild Goose strips. Press seams toward Ds.
4. To make block center section, join a C between 2 Wild Goose strips. Press seam allowances toward C.
5. Join 3 sections to complete each block. Make 16 blocks.

Quilt Top Assembly
1. Join blocks in 4 horizontal rows of 4 blocks each. Join rows.
2. Join a brown strip to each border print strip.
3. Mark center of each border on edge of brown fabric. Mark center on each edge of quilt top.
4. Matching centers of borders and quilt top, join borders to top and bottom edges. Add borders to quilt sides in same manner. See page 151 for tips on mitering border corners.

Quilting and Finishing
Outline-quilt patchwork and borders. If desired, quilt perpendicular lines through centers of each block that cross in the center of each C square.

  See page 157 for instructions on making and applying straight-grain binding.

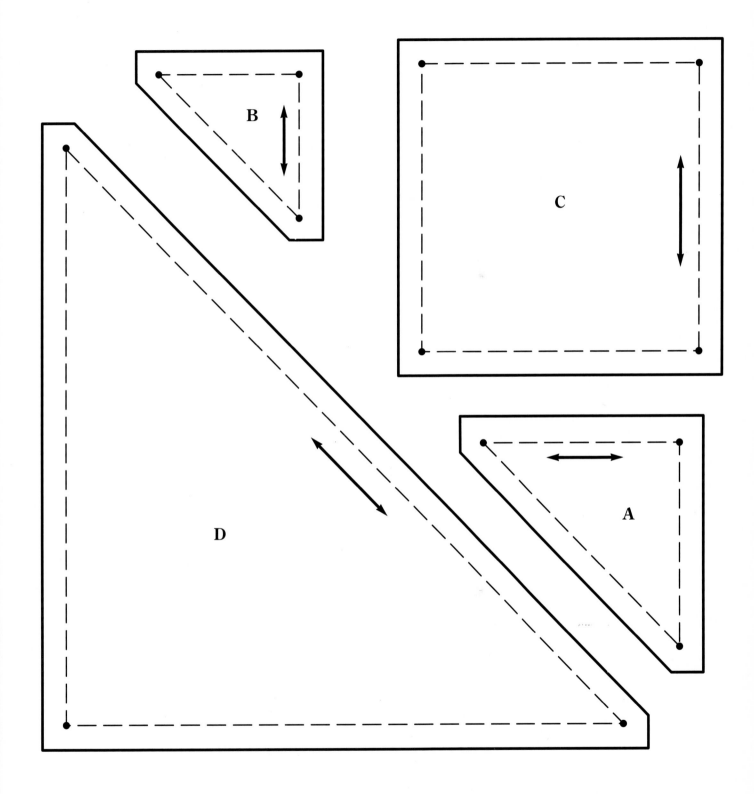

B

C

A

D

Ancient Greeks called
autumn "halcyon days,"
when the gods are kind.
The soft colors of
autumn's faded glory
make this an elegant
appliquéd quilt. The
space around its
graceful leafy vine can
showcase fine quilting.

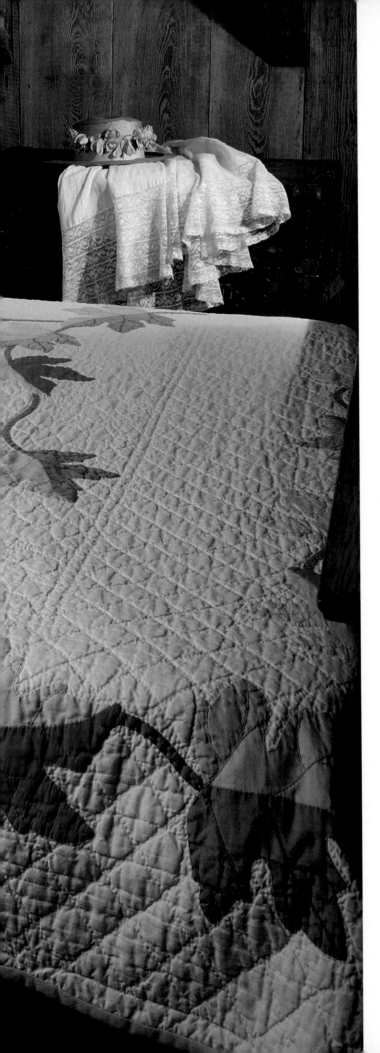

Halcyon Days

Finished Size: 73½" x 86"

Materials

2¼ yards of 90"-wide white sheeting (wide fabric is necessary to achieve economical cuts and to avoid seams through center section of quilt top)

¾ yard of dark green solid fabric

⅝ yard each of red and yellow solid fabrics

½ yard each of light green, tan, and brown solid fabrics

1 yard of blue fabric for binding

5 yards of backing fabric (or 2¼ yards of 90"-wide sheeting)

1 skein of embroidery floss to match each leaf fabric

Water-soluble marker or quilter's pencil

Cutting

1. See page 147 for tips on cutting bias. Cut a 19" square of dark green fabric into 1⅛"-wide bias strips of varying lengths for vines.

2. See page 145 for tips on making templates. Make finished-size templates for patterns A and B.

3. On right side of remaining dark green fabric, trace 4 As and 10 Bs. Cut appliqué pieces, adding seam allowances. Repeat to cut same number of pieces from brown fabric.

4. From each of the tan and light green fabrics, cut 10 As and 4 Bs.

5. Cut 2 As and 16 Bs from red fabric. Cut 16 yellow As and 2 yellow Bs.

6. Using water-soluble marker or quilter's pencil, trace embroidery lines on leaf pieces as shown on patterns.

7. From white sheeting, cut 2 (16½" x 75") border strips on lengthwise grain. Cut 2 (14" x 54½") crossgrain border strips.

8. From remaining white fabric, cut a 47" x 54½" rectangle for center panel.

Piecing and Appliqué

1. Join all yellow As to red Bs, referring to page 148 for tips on stitching curved seams. Machine-stitch center seam or, if you prefer, turn under the seam allowance of

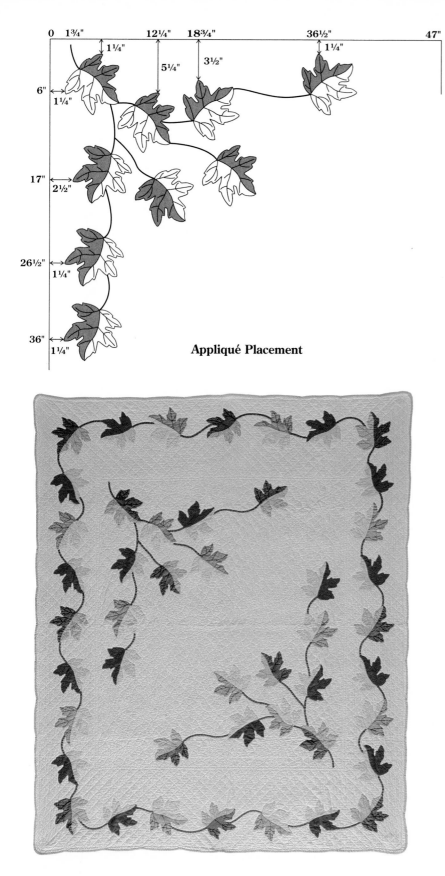

Appliqué Placement

1 piece and hand-appliqué pieces together. Make 16 yellow/red leaves; then join red As and yellow Bs to make 2 more leaves in the same manner.

2. Join 14 sets of brown and tan pieces and 14 sets of light and dark green pieces. Press seam allowances toward darker fabrics, clipping concave curves.

3. With wrong sides facing, fold 1 long edge of each green bias strip to center of strip and press. Fold opposite edge in same manner and press, making a finished strip approximately ⅜" wide.

4. Referring to Appliqué Placement diagram and photographs, pin leaves on center panel. Work out from top left corner and position leaves as shown. Cut lengths of bias as necessary and add vines between leaves, shaping bias as desired. Turn panel around and position leaves and vines in opposite corner in the same manner.

5. When satisfied with placement of leaves and vines on center panel, appliqué.

6. Join a 14" x 54½" border to each long side of center panel. Add remaining borders to top and bottom edges in same manner.

7. Find the center of each border strip. Referring to photograph for positioning, place the tip of a green leaf approximately 3" from the fabric edge at this point.

8. Referring to Border Corner Placement diagram and photograph, place green leaves at each border corner. Pin remaining leaves

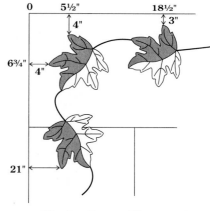

Border Corner Placement

on borders as shown; then add lengths of bias to make undulating vines between the leaves. Appliqué pieces in place on borders.

9. Use floss that matches leaf colors to embroider leaf veins in stem stitch.

Quilting and Finishing

Outline-quilt leaves, stems, and vines. Quilt 1½" cross-hatching over remainder of quilt.

See page 157 for tips on making and applying bias binding.

Spider Web

Finished Size
Block: 18 blocks, 11¼" x 13", and 4 half-blocks
Quilt: 63" x 67¼"

Materials
6 yards of black solid fabric (includes backing
  and binding)
1¾ yards of orange solid fabric
1 yard of black Halloween print fabric

Cutting
1. See page 145 for tips on making templates. Make templates of patterns A, B, and C. Mark horizontal placement lines on templates A and C.
2. Cut 2 (2-yard) lengths of black fabric. From each piece, cut a 33"-wide panel for backing. From remainder, cut 4 (4½" x 70") strips for outer borders.
3. For patchwork, cut 24 (2" x 42") crossgrain strips from each solid fabric.
4. From remaining orange fabric, cut 6 (2" x 42") strips for inner borders.
5. Cut 4 (6⅜" x 42") crossgrain strips of print fabric. From these, cut 34 As and 12 Cs as follows. Cut 3 strips as illustrated in Cutting diagram, rotating A template as shown and turning C template over to cut a reversed piece. Cut 4th strip in same manner, stopping at 7 As; then use leftover fabric to cut extra Cs and Cs reversed.

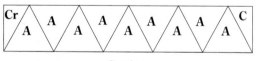
Cutting

6. From remaining print fabric, cut 22 Bs.

Piecing
1. Sew a black strip to both long sides of an orange strip. Repeat to make 8 pieced strip sets. Press seam allowances toward black fabric.
2. Referring to Diagram 1, position Template C at 1 end of 1 strip set, aligning template's bottom and straight side with edges of strip set. Placement lines on template should align with seams. The template's top point will extend past edge of strip set. Cut 1 C.

Diagram 1

Diagram 2

3. Position Template A with its bottom at the opposite fabric edge, aligning diagonal edges of template and fabric. Cut 1 A. Rotate template as shown in Diagram 1 to cut 6 more As, ending with a C reversed piece.
4. Follow steps 2 and 3 to cut 1 more strip set. For remaining 6 strip sets, eliminate Cs and cut only As as shown in Diagram 2. When all 8 strip sets are cut, you should have 58 A wedges (and 4 extras), 2 Cs, and 2 Cs reversed.
5. Join remaining solid strips, sewing a black strip between 2 orange ones to make 8 more strip sets. Follow steps 2–4 to cut same number of As and Cs.
6. Join an orange-black-orange A wedge to 1 side of a B hexagon. Be careful not to stitch into the seam allowance at each end of this seam. Referring to Block Assembly diagram, join a black-orange-black A wedge to B; then stitch seam to join adjacent As. Continue adding As of alternating strip sets around B in this manner. Make 18 blocks.

Block Assembly

7. Referring to Partial Blocks Assembly diagrams, use remaining A wedges and C wedges to make 2 of each partial block shown. Trim excess fabric from each B hexagon to align with raw edges of adjacent Cs.

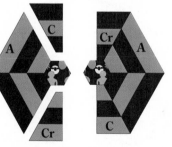
Partial Blocks Assembly

Mix the traditional
Spider Web design with
the marvelous novelty
prints available in today's
fabric stores to make a
fun and easy holiday wall
hanging or throw.
Add our bat quilting
designs for an
extra touch of Boo!

Trick or treat! For party favors or outstanding give-aways, children can decorate their own sacks and treat bags.

Halloween Treat Bags

Materials

Paper Treat Sacks
Brown paper lunch bags
4" x 7" translucent template plastic
Orange and black acrylic paints and paintbrush
¼"-diameter hole punch
Orange and black curling ribbon
Craft knife and scissors
Black broad-tipped marker (optional)

Canvas Candy Tote
½ yard each of canvaslike tan woven fabric and black
    Halloween print fabric
5" x 10" scrap of black solid fabric
5" x 10" piece each of paper-backed fusible web and
    tear-away stabilizer for machine appliqué
Orange fabric paint pen

Paper Treat Sacks

1. Trace small bat pattern onto template plastic. Use craft knife to cut out bat shape.
2. Paint bats in rows or random patterns on lunch bags.

Wipe stencil after each application to avoid smudges when positioning it to paint next bat. Let paint dry. If desired, outline orange bats with black marker.
3. Using contrasting color paint, dot eyes on bats.
4. Fill bags with goodies. Fold down top edges of each bag 1". In center of fold, punch 2 holes ½" apart.
5. Cut 4 (30") lengths of ribbon for each bag. Thread ribbons through holes and tie at front. To curl, place ribbon between your thumb and scissors blade; then pull scissors along ribbon.

Canvas Candy Tote

Note: The following instructions are for machine appliqué as shown. To hand appliqué, add seam allowances to bat pattern and disregard references to fusible web and tear-away stabilizer.

1. From tan and print fabrics, cut 17" x 37" rectangles.
2. On paper side of fusible web, trace Large Bat Quilting Design on page 88. Fuse web to wrong side of black fabric. Cut out bat. Peel paper from web.
3. Mark center of 37" side of tan rectangle. Center bat here, 3½" below edge. Fuse bat in place. Pin stabilizer to wrong side of fabric under bat. Machine satin-stitch around bat. Remove stabilizer.
4. With right sides facing, join 17" edges with a ½" seam allowance. Align seam with center front; then stitch bottom edges. Do not turn bag to right side.
5. To make squared bottom, align bottom seam with side fold to form a triangle as shown in Bag Bottom diagram. Pin bottom and side together 2" from tip of triangle. Stitch across base of triangle. Repeat for opposite corner. Trim triangles ½" from seam.

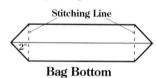

6. Repeat steps 4 and 5 to prepare lining.
7. For handles, cut 2 (2¼" x 18") strips of tan fabric and 2 (1¼" x 18") strips of print fabric. With right sides facing, join long edges of 1 tan strip and 1 print strip to make a tube. Turn to right side and press, centering print fabric. Repeat for second handle. Topstitch long edges of black fabric on both handles.
8. Mark 3" on each side of both center front and back seam. With right sides facing and raw edges aligned, baste ends of handles over placement marks.
9. At top edges of bag and lining, press ⅝" to wrong side. Insert lining into tote, with wrong sides facing. Match seams and center fronts; pin top edges together. Topstitch ¼" from edge through both layers. Repeat topstitching ¼" below first line.
10. Use paint pen to write desired message on tote.

Maple Leaf

Maple sap runs sweet in autumn, when there's a nip in the air and first frosts glisten on ripening pumpkins. Quick piecing techniques make it easier than ever to piece this time-honored version of a favorite autumn leaf.

Maple Leaf

Finished Size
Blocks: 30 blocks, 14" square
Quilt: 82" x 96"

Materials
4¾ yards of muslin
2½ yards of red print fabric for borders and binding
½ yard each of 10 assorted blue, red, and cranberry print fabrics
5¾ yards of backing fabric (or 2⅞ yards of 90"-wide sheeting)

Cutting
Note: Cutting instructions for triangles differ for traditional and quick piecing. Directions for cutting triangles are given with instructions for each technique.
1. See page 145 for tips on making templates. Make a template for A. Or, if you prefer, use an acrylic ruler and a rotary cutter to measure and cut each A square.
2. From each print fabric, cut and set aside an 8" x 42" piece for triangles and a 3" x 18" piece for stems. From remainder of each print fabric, cut 39 As.
3. Cut 35 (2½" x 42") strips of muslin. From these, cut 120 (2½" x 6½") strips for block crossbars and 240 As.
4. Cut 4 (6½" x 86") strips of border fabric.

Traditional Piecing
1. Make template for Pattern B. Cut 480 Bs from muslin and 48 Bs from each print fabric.
2. Join print Bs to muslin Bs to make 480 triangle-squares. Press seam allowances toward print fabrics.
3. For stems, cut each 3" x 18" print fabric in half lengthwise to make 2 (1½" x 18") strips. Fold each strip in half lengthwise, with wrong sides facing, and stitch a scant ¼" seam. Press seam allowances open and to center back of strip. Trim seam allowances if necessary. Cut each strip into 6 (3"-long) segments to make 12 stems of each fabric.
4. Center each stem diagonally on right side of muslin square. Appliqué or top-stitch stem in place as shown on A pattern.
5. Follow Piecing diagram to join A squares and pieced triangle-squares, making 3 horizontal rows for each block. Join

Piecing

rows to complete each leaf. Make 12 leaves from each print fabric.
6. Referring to Block Assembly diagram, join leaves in pairs with a muslin crossbar between them. Press seam allowances toward crossbars.
7. Join 2 crossbars with a print A square between them as shown. Press seam allowances toward crossbars.
8. Join leaf sections and center crossbar section as shown in Block Assembly diagram. Make 30 blocks.

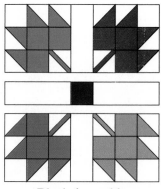

Block Assembly

Quick Piecing
1. Cut 3 (8" x 14") pieces from each print fabric and 30 matching pieces of muslin.
2. On the wrong side of each muslin piece, draw a 2 x 4-square grid of 2⅞" squares. Draw diagonal lines through squares as shown in Triangle-Square Grid diagram.

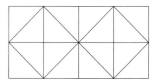

Triangle-Square Grid

3. Match print and muslin fabrics, with right sides facing and marked grid faceup. Following directions for half-square triangles on page 149, machine-stitch 30 grids. Cut 16 triangle-squares from each grid.
4. Follow steps 3–8 under Traditional Piecing to complete blocks.

Quilt Top Assembly
Referring to photograph, join blocks in 6 horizontal rows of 5 blocks each. Join rows.

Add border strips to long sides of quilt top. Press seam allowances toward borders; then trim borders even with quilt top as necessary. Join borders to top and bottom edges in the same manner.

Quilting and Finishing
Outline-quilt patchwork; then quilt borders as desired.

Use remaining border fabric for binding. See page 157 for directions on making and applying binding.

Maple Leaf Pot Holders

Finished Size: 8" x 8"

Materials (for 3 pot holders)
½ yard of muslin
Scraps or ¼ yard each of 3 print fabrics
½ yard of fleece or batting

Instructions

1. Set aside 3 (9") muslin squares for backing, 12 (1½" x 9") muslin strips for block borders, and a 2¼" x 42" strip of each print fabric for binding.
2. See directions for Maple Leaf block on page 92. Cut 3 As and 4 Bs of each print fabric. From remaining muslin, cut 6 As and 12 Bs.
3. Make a Maple Leaf block with each print fabric.
4. Join muslin border strips to top and bottom edges of each block. Trim ends of strips even with block; then press seam allowances toward border. Add side borders in same manner.
5. Sandwich 2 (9") squares of batting between a pieced block (faceup) and a muslin backing square. Pin layers together. Machine-quilt in-the-ditch of patchwork and borders.
6. See page 157 for tips on making and applying binding. Begin and end binding at a corner, leaving a 4½" tail at the end.
7. Turn binding to back of pot holder and blindstitch binding in place, starting with raw edges of tail and working around pot holder to starting point. As stitching approaches corner, tuck end of tail under binding to form loop; then finish blindstitching.

Add down-home flair to holiday meals and gifts with patchwork pot holders. Use our Maple Leaf or another 7" block with these finishing instructions.

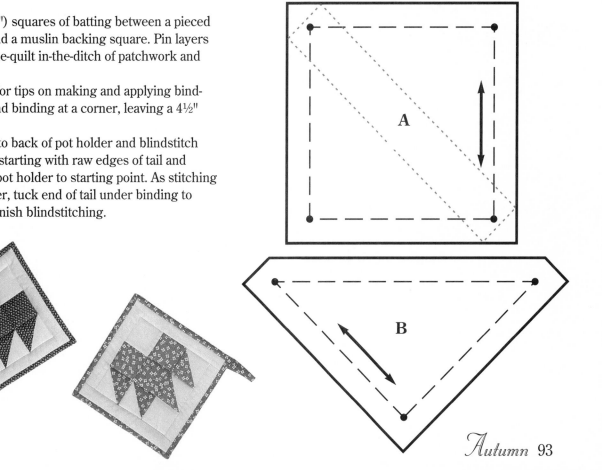

Use real leaves, in all their wondrous variety, as templates to make this radiant tribute to autumn's brilliance. Appliqué leaves helter-skelter and then quilt wavy lines of gusty wind.

Winds of Autumn

Finished Size: 86" x 109"

Materials

3⅛ yards of forest green solid fabric

2¾ yards of gold solid fabric

2½ yards of red solid fabric (includes binding)

1⅝ yards of 90"-wide muslin (wide fabric is necessary to avoid seams through center section of quilt top)

Scraps of 17 print fabrics in red, tan, brown, rust, yellow, gold, and dark green

7¼ yards of backing fabric (or 3¼ yards of 90"-wide sheeting)

Cutting

1. See page 145 for tips on making templates for appliqué. When Barbara White of Newark, Delaware, made this quilt, she collected 17 leaves from which she made templates. She stylized the leaves to remove small, sharp points that are difficult to appliqué. We've included patterns (on this page and pages 96 and 97) for 6 of Barbara's leaves. Collect as many leaves of different shapes and sizes as you like. Make a finished-size template for each leaf.

2. Trace each leaf template on right side of selected print fabric, marking quilting lines for veins on each leaf. Adding seam allowances, cut 85 leaves, approximately 5 of each fabric.

3. From remaining scraps, cut short 1"-wide bias strips to make a stem for each leaf.

4. For center panel, cut a 58" x 81" piece of muslin.

5. For red inner border, cut 2 (4" x 66") strips and 2 (4" x 89") strips.

6. For gold middle border, cut 2 (5½" x 76") strips and 2 (5½" x 99") strips.

7. For green outer border, cut 2 (6½" x 88") strips and 2 (6½" x 111") strips.

Appliqué

Turn under seam allowances on leaves and stems. Pin pieces on muslin, placing different colors and shapes randomly. Keep leaves at least 2½" from muslin edges. Stems should underlap leaves at least ¼". Appliqué all pieces in place.

Quilt Top Assembly

1. Mark centers on edges of all border strips.

2. Matching centers, join 2 sets of long border strips with a gold strip between red and green strips. Make 2 sets of short border strips in same manner.

3. Mark centers on quilt top edges. Matching centers of borders and quilt top, join long borders to side edges. Add short borders to top and bottom edges. See page 151 for tips on mitering border corners.

Quilting and Finishing

Barbara used a specific leaf for a quilting design in each border, tumbled about by wavy lines of quilting to indicate autumn winds. We've included a pattern for the inner border corner (on page 97) to get you started. Barbara used Leaf F here, turning it helter-skelter, and drawing undulating lines between each leaf. She used Leaf B in the middle border and Leaf C in the outer border. Mark quilting designs in borders as desired.

Quilt veins in each leaf; then outline-quilt leaves. Add wavy lines of quilting around appliquéd leaves to create the impression of leaves tumbling in the wind.

Use remaining red fabric to make binding. See page 157 for instructions on making and applying binding.

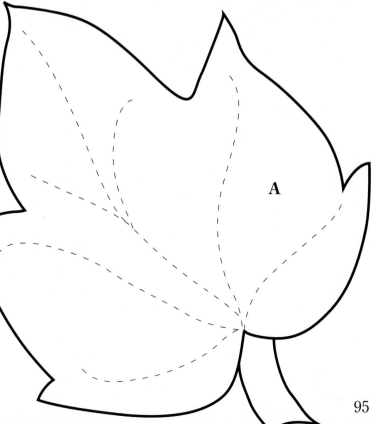

C

B

E

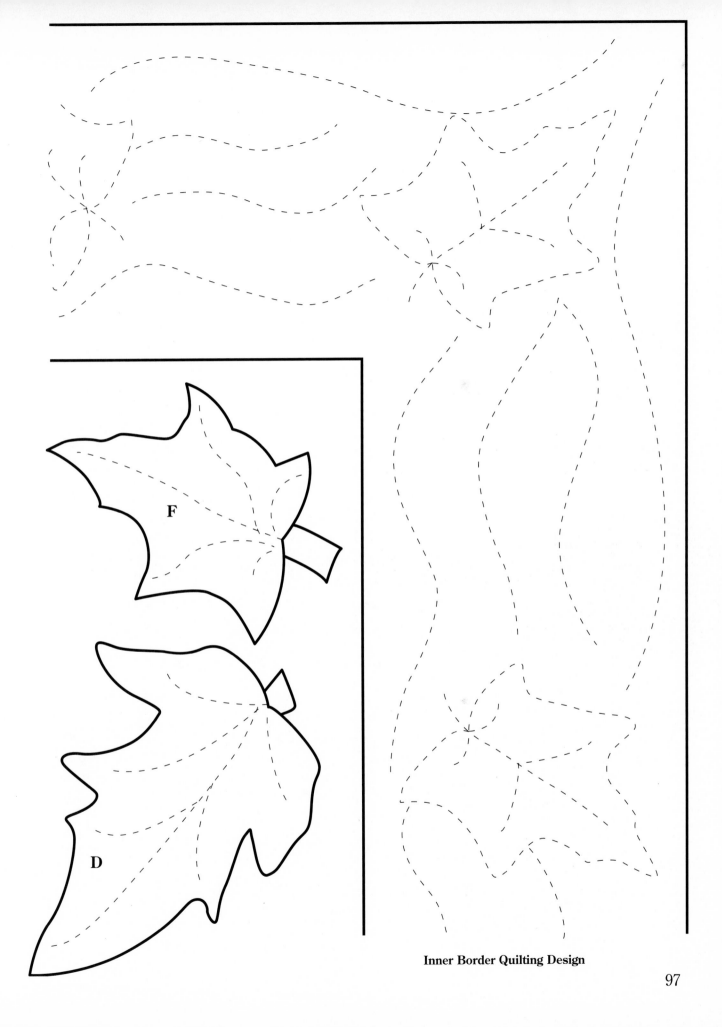

Inner Border Quilting Design

Days grow short as Mother Earth prepares for a season of slumber, and brown is the dye of her dress. Rich brown, the color of earth, adds warmth to this quilt, made fast and easy with shortcut instructions.

Repeating Crosses

Finished Size
Blocks: 42 blocks, 12" square
Quilt: 89" x 101"

Materials
4 yards each of cream and brown print fabrics
3 yards of brown solid fabric for unpieced inner and
    outer borders (or 1⅛ yards for pieced borders)
2½ yards of brown floral print for unpieced middle
    border (or 1⅝ yards for pieced borders)
1 yard of binding fabric
8¼ yards of backing fabric (or 2¾ yards of 108"-wide
    sheeting)

Cutting
1. Cut 68 (2" x 42") crossgrain strips each from cream
print and brown print fabrics.
2. For inner border, cut 2 (2" x 77") strips and 2
(2" x 86") strips of brown solid fabric. (To piece these
borders, cut 2"-wide crossgrain strips and piece strips
end-to-end to make borders of needed length.)
3. For outer border, cut or piece 2 (2" x 91") strips and
2 (2" x 100") strips of brown solid fabric.
4. For middle border, cut or piece 4 (6" x 90") strips.

Piecing
1. See page 145 for tips on making templates. Make
Triangle A template. Mark placement line on template.
2. Join a cream strip and a brown print strip.
3. Referring to Cutting diagram, place template on strip,
aligning horizontal line with seam. Cut 1 Triangle A.

Cutting

4. Turn template upside-down, aligning long
edge with opposite edge of fabric and
placement line with seam line. Cut second
Triangle A as shown. Continue, cutting
10 As from strip set.

5. Repeat steps 2–4 with each pair of strips to make 672
As. Make separate stacks of brown/cream As and
cream/brown As.
6. Matching short sides, join 2
brown/cream As to make a triangle. Repeat with 2 cream/brown
As. Referring to Block Assembly
diagram, join triangles.
7. Make 4 squares for each block.
Position squares as shown to complete block. Make 42 blocks.

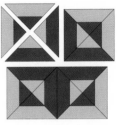

Block Assembly

Quilt Top Assembly
1. Arrange blocks in 7 horizontal rows of 6 blocks each.
Join blocks in rows; then join rows.
2. Join 2" x 86" brown borders to sides of quilt top.
Press seam allowances toward borders. Trim borders
even with quilt edges. Add 2" x 77" borders to top and
bottom edges.
3. Add middle and outer borders in same manner, joining long borders to sides first and then joining
shorter border strips to top and bottom edges.

Quilting and Finishing
Outline-quilt patchwork and borders
or quilt as desired. See page 157
for instructions on making and
applying binding.

A

Indian Trails

Finished Size
Blocks: 15 blocks, 12" square
Quilt: 73" x 85"

Materials
3¼ yards of osnaburg or muslin
2½ yards of cranberry solid fabric for borders and binding
1 yard each of cranberry print, earth-tone print, and olive green print fabrics
5 yards of backing fabric (or 2½ yards of 90"-wide sheeting)

Cutting
Note: Cutting instructions for some pieces differ for traditional piecing and quick piecing. The following instructions are for those pieces that are cut the same way for both methods. Additional cutting instructions are given with directions for each technique.

1. See page 145 for tips on making templates. Make template for C.
2. Cut 15 (12½") setting squares of osnaburg.
3. From osnaburg, cut 3 (2" x 42") strips. From these, cut 60 (2") squares for Cs.
4. For border, cut 2 (7" x 74") strips and 2 (7" x 86") strips of cranberry solid fabric.

Traditional Piecing
1. Make templates for A and B.
2. Cut 60 As each from cranberry and earth-tone print fabrics. Join As in pairs, making 60 triangle-squares. Press seam allowances toward earth-tone print.
3. Cut 360 Bs each from osnaburg and green print fabric. Join Bs in pairs, making 360 triangle-squares. Press seam allowances toward green fabric.

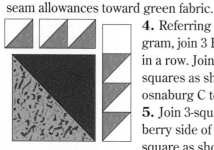

Piecing

4. Referring to Piecing diagram, join 3 B triangle-squares in a row. Join 3 more B triangle-squares as shown, adding an osnaburg C to 1 end.
5. Join 3-square unit to cranberry side of an A triangle-square as shown; then add 4-square unit to other cranberry side. Press seam allowances toward A.

6. Make 4 squares for each block. Referring to Block Assembly diagram, position squares as shown and join to complete block. Make 15 blocks.

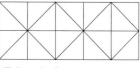

Block Assembly

Quilt Assembly

Quick Piecing
1. From both earth-tone print and cranberry print, cut 3 (14" x 30") pieces. On wrong side of each earth-tone piece, draw a 2 x 5-square grid of 5⅜" squares. Draw diagonal lines through each

Triangle-Square Grid A

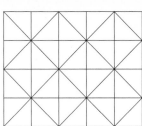

Celebrating the bounty of autumn's harvest is an ancient, treasured American tradition. Good food, good friends, and a warm quilt stitched with love is truly reason for Thanksgiving.

square as shown in Triangle-Square Grid A.

2. Match each earth-tone piece with a cranberry print piece, with right sides facing and marked grid faceup.

3. Following directions for half-square triangles on page 149, machine-stitch grids. Cut grids apart to make 20 triangle-squares from each grid.

4. From both osnaburg and green print, cut 9 (12" x 14") pieces. On wrong side of each osnaburg piece, draw a 4 x 5-square grid of 2⅜" squares. Draw diagonal lines through each square as shown in Triangle-Square Grid B. Stitch and cut these 9 grids as

before, making 40 triangle-squares from each grid.

5. Follow steps 4–6 for traditional piecing to join block units. Make 15 blocks.

Quilt Top Assembly

1. Referring to Quilt Assembly diagram, arrange blocks and osnaburg setting squares in 6 horizontal rows of 5 blocks each. Join blocks in rows; then join rows.

Triangle-Square Grid B

2. Matching centers of quilt side and border, join a 7" x 86" border strip to each long side of quilt top. Press seam allowances toward borders. Add 7" x 74" borders to top and bottom edges. See page 151 for tips on mitering border corners.

Quilting and Finishing

Lay quilt top on a flat surface for marking. See page 153 for tips on making stencils of full-size quilting designs. Referring to photograph and Quilt Assembly diagram, mark Leaf and Acorn design in setting squares. Mark Oak Leaf design in borders.

   Outline-quilt patchwork. Quilt setting squares and borders as marked.

   Use remaining border fabric for binding. See page 157 for instructions on making and applying binding.

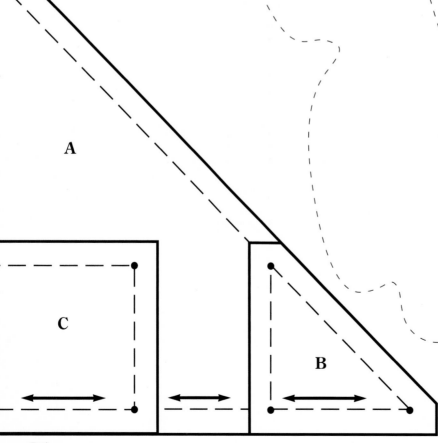

Half of pattern

Oak Leaf Quilting Design

Leaf and Acorn Quilting Design

Winter

Whose woods these are I think I know.
    His house is in the village, though;
He will not see me stopping here
    To watch his woods fill up with snow.
My little horse must think it queer
    To stop without a farmhouse near
Between the woods and frozen lake
    The darkest evening of the year.
He gives his harness bells a shake
    To ask if there is some mistake.
The only other sound's the sweep
    Of easy wind and downy flake. . . .

Robert Frost,
"Stopping By Woods on a Snowy Evening"

Winter's quilts translate the colors of the
season with fabrics of icy blue, berry red, holly
green, deepest ebony, and sparkling white.
While burning logs snap and crackle on the
hearth, spend this season of slumber embraced
in the warmth of home and the pleasure of creating beautiful quilts.

Like constellations ablaze in the inky dark of winter skies, pieced stars shine brightly in this classic patchwork setting. Use different colors in the Garden Maze sashing to alter the season of the quilt's personality.

Stars Over My Garden Maze

Finished Size

Blocks: 12 blocks, 12" square
Quilt: 74" x 93½"

Materials

3 yards of floral print fabric for maze and star centers
3 yards of navy print fabric for maze and binding
2¾ yards of beige miniprint fabric for outer border and block corners
1 yard of striped fabric for blocks
¼ yard of red miniprint fabric for inner border
Scraps or 18" square each of 8 print fabrics for blocks (dark blue, brown, and red)
5¾ yards of backing fabric (or 2⅞ yards of 90"-wide sheeting)

Cutting

1. See page 145 for tips on making templates. Make templates for patterns A–H.
2. From 1 yard of floral print fabric, cut 96 As (8 for each star block). *Note:* Some florals, like the one used in this quilt, can be cut to create a kaleidoscopic effect in the center of a star. Arleen Boyd of Rochester, NY, made this quilt using a single fabric for the star centers; but, by positioning her template judiciously, Arleen cut pieces for 12 stars that look very different. (See block photo.) If you try this technique, pay close attention to template placement on your fabric, positioning the same flowers in the same manner for 8 As in each star. Yardage allows extra fabric for experimentation and selective template placement.

2. Join a GFG triangle to both sides of each H piece to complete 20 sashing squares.

3. For sashing strips, join a 2" x 50" navy strip to both sides of each 5" x 50" floral strip. Referring to Sashing Strip Assembly diagram, cut 4 (12½"-long) segments from each strip set.

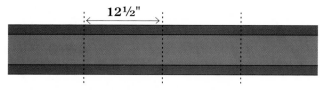

Sashing Strip Assembly

Quilt Top Assembly

1. Referring to Quilt Assembly diagram, arrange blocks in 4 horizontal rows of 3 blocks each with sashing strips between. Join blocks and sashing strips in each row.

Add sashing strips to ends of rows. Press seam allowances toward sashing.

2. To make each horizontal sashing row, join 4 sashing squares and 3 sashing strips as shown. Make 5 sashing rows. Press seam allowances toward sashing strips.

3. Follow Quilt Assembly diagram to join block rows and sashing rows.

4. Join 2 (¾" x 42") red strips end-to-end to make borders for top and bottom edges. Join 3 strips for sides.

5. Mark centers on edges of each red and beige border strip. Matching centers, join red and beige strips in pairs. Trim red borders to match length of beige borders. Repeat for long border strips.

6. Mark centers on edges of quilt top. Matching centers of borders and quilt top, join shorter borders to top and bottom edges. Add long borders to sides in same manner. See page 151 for tips on mitering border corners.

Quilting and Finishing

Outline-quilt block patchwork and inner border. Quilt straight lines in dark blue sashing pieces, parallel to seams and spaced ½" apart. Quilt diagonal cross-hatching in floral print sashing pieces, spacing lines ⅝" apart.

Quilt straight lines in beige border, perpendicular to seams and spaced 1" apart.

See page 157 for instructions on making and applying bias or straight-grain binding.

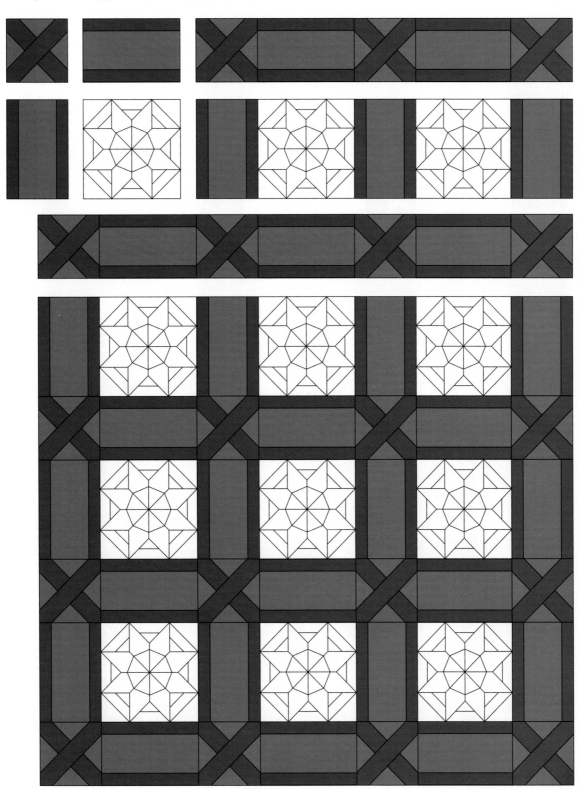

Quilt Assembly

2. Trace 5 angel halos onto paper side of a 5" x 9" piece of fusible web. Following manufacturer's directions, fuse web to wrong side of interfaced lamé. Cut out 5 halos, following traced lines on web. Remove paper backing.

3. In same manner, trace 5 angels (without halos) onto fusible web. Cut web between angels. Fuse web pieces to wrong side of a 10" square of green solid fabric. Cut out pieces; then remove paper backings.

4. Center pieces for 1 angel on a pindot square. (If desired, lightly trace pattern on fabric to aid in placement.) Fuse pieces in place. Repeat to make 5 angel squares.

5. Pin an 11" square of stabilizer to wrong side of fabric under each appliqué.

Machine Appliqué

Thread sewing machine with metallic thread on top and white thread in bobbin. Adjust stitch to make a medium-width satin stitch. Appliqué around angel pieces.

Tear stabilizer away from stitching when appliqué is complete. Press wrong side of each square.

Quilt Top Assembly

1. Position each remaining background square over star pattern on page 117, matching centers of fabric and pattern. Lightly trace star and rays on fabric. Or, if you prefer, make a quilting stencil with which to mark design on fabric.

2. Referring to Quilt Assembly diagram on page 112, arrange blocks in 3 vertical rows of 3 squares each.

3. Join blocks in rows with 2¼" x 10½" sashing strips between blocks as shown. Press seam allowances toward sashing.

4. Join rows with 34" lengthwise sashing strips between them.

5. Join crosswise green print border strips to top and bottom edges; then add side borders. Join solid green strips in same manner for middle border.

6. Join gold-on-green borders to quilt top for outer border. See page 151 for tips on mitering corners.

Quilting and Finishing

Use metallic thread to quilt marked stars by hand or by machine. Outline-quilt seam lines of blocks and sashing strips. Quilt borders as desired. Use remaining green solid fabric to make straight-grain binding. See page 157 for instructions on making and applying binding.

Christmas Pillows

Finished Size
Angel Pillow, 14" square
Star Pillow, 12" square plus 2½"-wide ruffle

Materials
Angel Pillow
½ yard of green print fabric
10½" square of gold-on-white pindot fabric
10" square of green solid fabric
Scrap of gold lamé
15" square each of batting and lining material
10" square each of paper-backed fusible web and
   tear-away stabilizer for machine appliqué
1¾ yards of ¼"-wide cording
Gold metallic thread and clear monofilament thread
14" square pillow form

Star Pillow
⅞ yard of gold-on-green stripe or print fabric
10½" square of gold-on-white pindot fabric
7" x 13" piece of green solid fabric
9" x 11" piece of gold lamé
14" square each of batting and lining material
9" x 11" piece of 100%-cotton fusible interfacing
10" square each of paper-backed fusible web and
   tear-away stabilizer for machine appliqué
Gold metallic thread
12" square pillow form

Angel Pillow

1. From green print fabric, cut 2 (11" x 15") pieces for pillow back. From remaining green print fabric, cut 2 (2¾" x 15") lengthwise strips and 2 (2¾" x 10½") cross-grain strips for borders.

2. Follow instructions for wall quilt to prepare and cut pieces for 1 angel from pindot, lamé, and green solid fabric. Machine-appliqué angel as directed.

3. Join 10½"-long green print strips to top and bottom edges of pindot square. Add remaining borders to sides.

4. Sandwich batting between pillow top and lining. Using gold thread, machine-quilt around each angel piece, in-the-ditch along border seams, and ¼" from seam on green border fabric. Baste edge to secure layers. Pillow top should measure 15" square.

5. On 1 long edge of each back piece, press under ¼". On same edges, turn under 1½" more and hem.

Make decorative pillows with glitzy lamé, sparkling braid, and cheery Christmas fabrics to spread holiday style throughout the house.

6. With right sides up and hemmed edges overlapped, position back pieces to make a 15" square. To secure, baste raw edges at top and bottom where hems overlap.

7. With right sides facing and using a ½" seam, join pillow top and back, leaving a ¾" opening at bottom center. Clip corners; then turn pillow right side out.

8. Insert ½" cording into opening. Using monofilament, hand-stitch cording along seam. Insert last ½" of cording into opening. From wrong side, machine-sew opening closed, securing cording tails. Insert pillow form.

Star Pillow

1. From gold-on-green fabric, cut 3 (6" x 42") strips for ruffle and 2 (9" x 13") pieces for pillow back. From solid green fabric, cut 4 (1¾" x 13") border strips.

2. Follow instructions for wall quilt to preshrink interfacing and fuse it to wrong side of lamé.

3. Trace star pattern on page 117 on paper side of fusible web. Following manufacturer's directions, fuse web to wrong side of interfaced lamé. Cut out star.

4. Follow instructions for wall quilt to prepare pindot square. Machine-appliqué around outside edge of star.

5. Join borders to top and bottom of square. Trim even with sides. Add remaining borders to sides.

6. Sandwich batting between pillow top and lining fabric. Using gold thread, machine-quilt detail lines inside star and light rays on each side. Quilt in-the-ditch along border seams and ¼" from seam on borders. Baste edge to secure layers. Pillow top should measure 13" square.

7. For back, repeat steps 5 and 6 for Angel Pillow to make a 13" square.

8. Join ruffle strips end-to-end to make 1 (125"-long) strip. At 1 end, fold back a 1½" hem. With wrong sides facing, press strip in half lengthwise. Run a gathering thread ¼" from raw edge. Gather ruffle to fit pillow top.

9. With raw edges aligned, pin ruffle to right side of pillow top. Overlap ends 2" and trim excess. Tuck raw end inside folded end. Baste ruffle to pillow top.

10. With right sides facing and using a ½" seam, join pillow top and back. Clip corners; then turn pillow right side out. Insert pillow form.

Angel Pattern

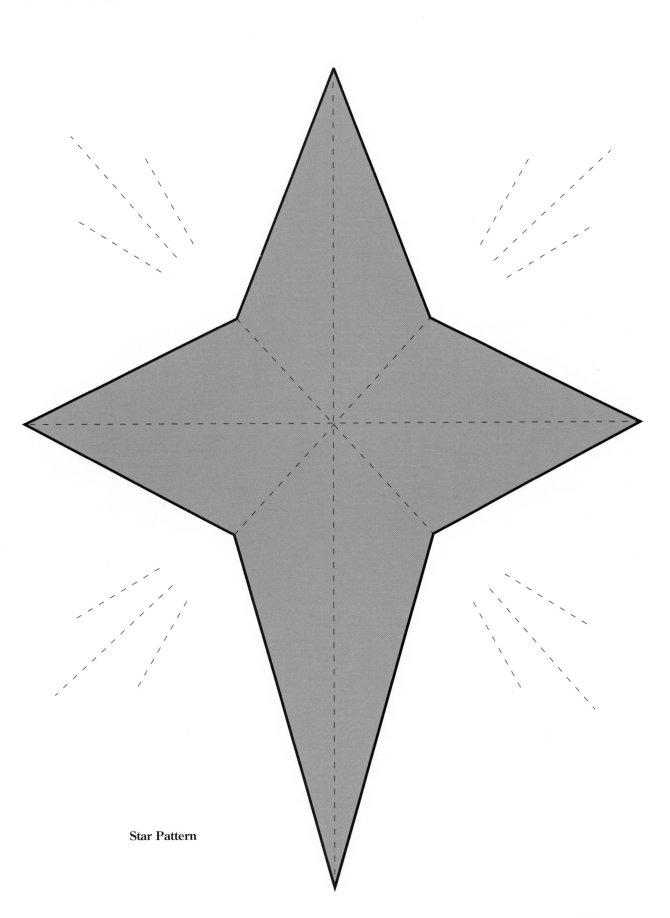

Star Pattern

The connecting pathways of this charming patchwork are like berries on a field of gleaming snow. With timesaving techniques, you can finish the piecing between Christmas and New Year's Eve.

Stepping Stones

Finished Size
Blocks: 12 blocks, 16" square
Quilt: 82" x 100"

Materials
7¼ yards of muslin (includes binding)
3⅝ yards of cranberry print fabric
6 yards of backing fabric (or 3 yards of 90"-wide sheeting)

Cutting
Note: Cutting instructions for some pieces differ for traditional piecing and quick piecing. The following instructions are for those pieces that are cut the same way for both methods. Additional cutting instructions are given with directions for each technique.
1. See page 145 for tips on making templates. Make templates for patterns A, C, D, E, F, and G. Or, if you prefer, measure and cut pieces with an acrylic ruler and rotary cutter.
2. Set aside 1¼ yards of muslin and a ¾-yard piece of cranberry print fabric for blocks' As and Bs. Set aside ⅞ yard of muslin for binding.
3. Cut 2¾ yards of muslin for borders. From this, cut 2 (4½" x 98") strips, 2 (4½" x 84") strips, 2 (4½" x 72") strips, and 2 (4½" x 58") strips.
4. Cut a ⅝-yard length of muslin. From this, cut 200 Fs.
5. From remaining muslin, cut 16 (2½" x 42") strips. From these, cut 31 (2½" x 16½") strips for sashing. Use leftover fabric from these strips to cut 16 Gs.
6. From remaining muslin, cut 192 Cs.
7. For cranberry borders, cut 2 (2½" x 98") strips and 2 (2½" x 84") strips.
8. From remaining cranberry print fabric, cut 48 Ds, 48 Ds reversed, 12 Es, and 124 As for sashing and middle border.

Traditional Piecing
1. Make template for pattern B.
2. From fabric set aside for blocks, cut 96 As and 96 Bs from muslin; then cut 144 As from cranberry fabric.
3. Join a muslin A to 1 side of each cranberry A. Press seam allowances toward cranberry fabric.

4. Join 1 remaining cranberry A to 1 end of each B rectangle. Press seam allowances toward As.

5. Referring to Block Assembly diagram, join 2 A pairs to make a 4-patch unit. Make 4 of these units for each block. Add a B piece to 1 side of each 4-patch as shown. Press seam allowances toward As.

6. Join an AB unit to each 4-patch as shown.

7. Join Cs to both ends of each D and D reversed piece. Press seam allowances toward cranberry fabric. Join a CDC unit to each CDrC unit as shown. Make 4 units for each block.

8. Follow Block Assembly diagram to join an E square and pieced units in horizontal rows; then join rows. Make 12 blocks.

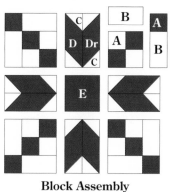

Block Assembly

Quick Piecing

If you're short of time or if marking and cutting just isn't your thing, take a shortcut to reduce marking, cutting, and sewing time. All block corner units can be quick-pieced.

1. From fabric set aside for blocks' As and Bs, cut 9 (2½" x 42½") strips of cranberry fabric and 6 matching strips of muslin. From remaining muslin, cut 6 (4½" x 42½") strips.

2. Join cranberry strips to all 2½"-wide muslin strips and 3 (4½"-wide) strips along 1 long edge. Press seam allowances toward cranberry fabric.

3. Referring to Quick Piecing/Cutting diagram, cut each strip set into 2½"-wide segments. Cut 16 segments from each strip set, making 96 AA units and 48 AB units.

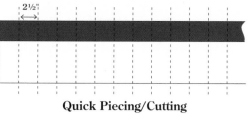

Quick Piecing/Cutting

4. Cut 3 remaining muslin strips in same manner to make 48 Bs.

5. Follow steps 5–8 under Traditional Piecing to complete blocks.

Quilt Top Assembly

1. Referring to Quilt Assembly diagram on page 122, arrange blocks in 4 horizontal rows of 3 blocks each with sashing strips between blocks. Join blocks and sashing strips in each row. Add sashing strips to ends of rows. Press seam allowances toward sashing.

2. To make each horizontal sashing row, join 4 cranberry A squares and 3 muslin sashing strips as shown. Make 5 sashing rows. Press seam allowances toward sashing strips.

3. Follow Quilt Assembly diagram to join block rows and sashing rows.

4. Join 4½" x 58" muslin borders to top and bottom edges of quilt top. Trim borders even with sides of quilt top; then press seam allowances toward borders.

5. Compare 4½" x 84" muslin borders to side edges of quilt. Trim borders to match sides, but do not join yet.

6. Referring to Border Piecing diagram, join remaining cranberry A squares with F and G triangles as shown to make each unit of the middle border. Using a scant ¼" seam, join 28 A

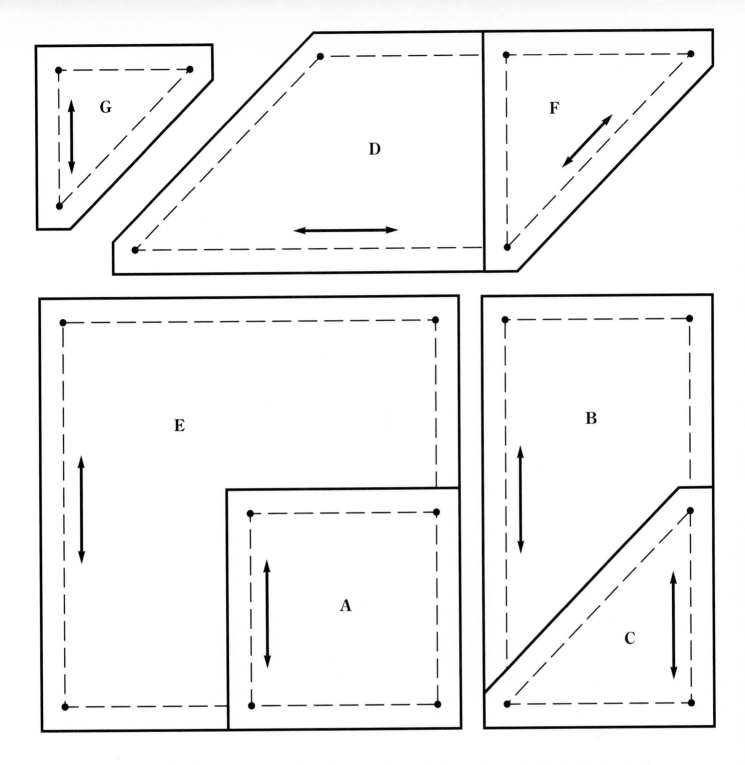

units for each side border. Compare length of pieced borders with trimmed muslin borders; then adjust piecing to make borders match.

Border Piecing

7. Join pieced side borders to muslin side borders. Referring to Quilt Assembly diagram, join side borders to quilt top.

8. Make 24 A units for each top and bottom border as for side borders. Adjust seams as necessary to match borders with width of quilt top. Referring to Quilt Assembly diagram, join pieced borders to top and bottom edges.

9. Join 4½" x 72" muslin borders to top and bottom edges of quilt top.

10. Matching long edges, join 96"-long cranberry borders and muslin borders. Add these pieced units to quilt sides as shown. Trim borders even with quilt top.

11. Add remaining cranberry borders to top and bottom edges of quilt top.

F
A
G

Quilt Assembly

Quilting and Finishing

Use a purchased stencil to mark a 3"-wide cable (or design of your choice) in muslin borders. Outline-quilt patchwork and sashing; then quilt marked borders.

See page 157 for instructions on making and applying binding.

122 *Winter*

Black Tie Affair

Toast the new year
wrapped in a quilt of
elegant black and white.
Use scraps of funky fabric
prints to add excitement
to piecing the classic
Bow Tie blocks.

Black Tie Affair

Finished Size

Blocks: 32 blocks, 12" square
Quilt: 84" x 101"

Materials

3⅛ yards of black solid fabric
2½ yards of red solid fabric for unpieced inner border
   (or ¾ yard for pieced border)
2¼ yards of white solid fabric
Scraps or ¼ yard each of 20 black-on-white print fabrics
   and 12 white-on-black print fabrics
1 yard of black striped fabric for binding
6¼ yards of backing fabric (or 3 yards of 90"-wide
   sheeting)

Cutting

1. See page 145 for tips on making templates. Make templates for patterns A and B.
2. From black solid fabric, cut 2 (6½" x 86") strips and 2 (6½" x 91") strips for outer borders.
3. From remaining black solid fabric, cut 40 As.
4. Cut 4 (18¼") squares of white solid fabric. Cut these in quarters diagonally to make 14 (and 2 extra) X setting triangles.
5. Cut 2 (9½") white squares. Cut these in half diagonally to make 4 Y corner triangles.
6. From remaining white fabric, cut 24 As.
7. From each scrap fabric, cut 2 As and 1 B.
8. For an unpieced red inner border, cut 2 (2½" x 74") strips and 2 (2½" x 87") strips. For a pieced border, cut 10 (2½" x 42") crossgrain strips and piece these strips as needed to equal lengths of lengthwise borders.

Piecing

1. Join black As to opposite sides of a white B. Be careful not to sew into seam allowance so that next pieces can be set in. Press seam allowances toward black fabric.
2. Referring to assembly diagram for Block 1, join 2 matching white print As to remaining sides of B square in the same manner; then stitch seams to join black As and white print As. Make 20 of Block 1.
3. Make 12 of Block 2, using white solid As and black print As as shown in Block Assembly diagram.

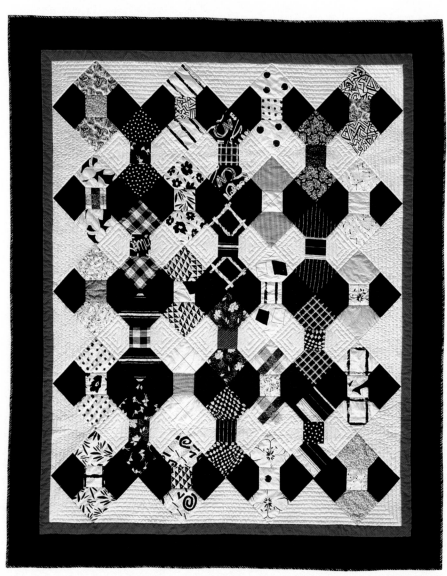

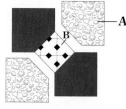

Block 1—Make 20
Block Assembly

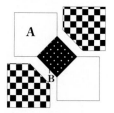

Block 2—Make 12
Block Assembly

Quilt Top Assembly

1. Join 2 Block 1s and 2 Block 2s as shown in 4-Block Unit diagram. Make 5 (4-block) units.

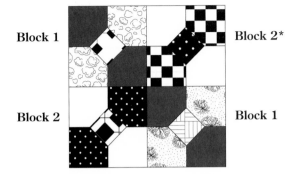

Block 1   **Block 2***

Block 2   **Block 1**

4-Block Unit

2. Make 2 more units, substituting a white X setting triangle for 1 of Block 2 (indicated by * in diagram).

3. Referring to Quilt Assembly diagram, combine remaining blocks with X setting triangles and Y corner triangles to make 4 corner units and 2 side units.

4. Arrange units in diagonal rows as indicated by red lines in diagram. Join units in each row, omitting corner units at bottom left and top right. Join rows to assemble quilt top, adding remaining corner units.

5. Join long red borders to sides of quilt top. Trim borders even with patchwork and press seam allowances toward borders. Add short red border strips to top and bottom of quilt top.

6. Join black borders to quilt top in same manner.

Quilting and Finishing

Make a stencil for Border Quilting Design on page 127. Mark corner section of quilting design (indicated in red) in each black A. White As are quilted as indicated on pattern—this design can be marked with a stencil or measured with a ruler. Mark Border Quilting Design in each corner of black border; then repeat long and short loops along each border as shown.

Quilt As as marked and outline-quilt B squares. Quilt red border as desired; then quilt marked black border.

See page 157 for tips on making and applying bias or straight-grain binding.

Quilt Assembly

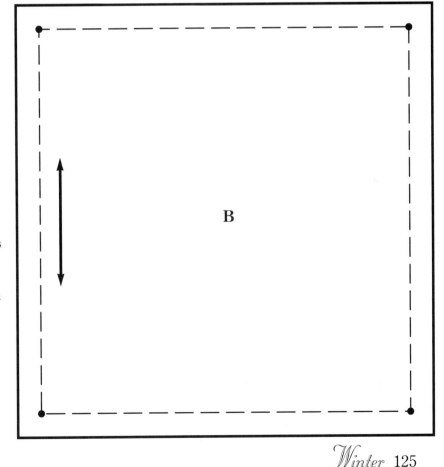

B

Winter Roses

Finished Size
Blocks: 12 blocks, 15" square
Quilt: 83" x 103"

Materials
5 yards of blue solid fabric (includes binding)
2¾ yards of muslin
2½ yards of blue-on-ivory toile or print fabric
1 yard of marble-look blue fabric
9¼ yards of backing fabric (or 3⅛ yards of 90"-wide
   sheeting)

Cutting
Note: The curves in this design are particularly appropriate for freezer-paper appliqué. See page 150 for an explanation of this technique. If you wish to use freezer paper, mark and cut appliqué pieces according to those instructions.

1. See page 145 for tips on making templates for appliqué. Make finished-size templates for patterns A–F.
2. Trace templates A and C on right side of marble-look fabric. Adding seam allowances, cut 12 As and 12 Cs.
3. Cut 4 (9½" x 87") blue solid border strips.
4. From remaining blue solid fabric, cut 12 Bs, 12 Ds, 48 Es, 48 Fs, and 48 Fs reversed.
5. From muslin, cut 12 (15½") squares.
6. For inner borders, cut 2 (5½" x 87") strips of toile on lengthwise grain and 4 (5½" x 29") crossgrain strips.
7. From remaining toile, cut 8 (5½" x 15½") strips on lengthwise grain (with long edge parallel to selvage) and 9 crossgrain strips of same size for sashing. Also cut 6 (5½") sashing squares.

Appliqué
1. Fold each muslin square in half vertically, horizontally, and diagonally, finger-pressing folds to make placement guidelines. Make placement guidelines on appliqué pieces A–D in same manner.
2. Turn under seam allowances on appliqué pieces. Leave E ends flat where they will be covered by As.
3. Pin an A on each square, matching centers. Then pin 4 Es on each square, aligning with diagonal placement lines and tucking flat ends under A.

In the cold of winter,
summer roses can bloom
fresh in our hearts and
minds. The flower of love,
a rose warms us inside
and out, whether pressed
between the pages of a
book or preserved in
appliqués of icy blue.

4. Pin an F and an F reversed on both sides of each E, placing leaves in middle of stem. Appliqué Es and Fs.
5. Appliqué As. Trim muslin behind As, leaving seam allowances.
6. Center Bs on As. Appliqué. Trim fabric behind Bs. Add Cs and Ds in same manner. Make 12 blocks.

Quilt Top Assembly

1. Refer to Quilt Assembly diagram to arrange blocks.
2. Join blocks in each row with sashing strips between.
3. Referring to diagram, piece 3 sashing rows.
4. Join rows, alternating sashing and block rows.

5. Join 2 (5½" x 29") toile strips end-to-end to make top and bottom inner border strips. Join borders to quilt. Trim borders even with quilt sides.
6. Referring to Quilt Assembly diagram, join 87" toile and blue border strips along 1 long edge. Join borders to quilt sides. Trim border ends even with quilt top.
7. Join remaining solid borders to top and bottom.

Quilting and Finishing

Outline-quilt leaves and rose layers. Quilt cross-hatching of 1" squares in sashing and borders. See page 157 for instructions on making and applying blue solid binding.

Quilt Assembly

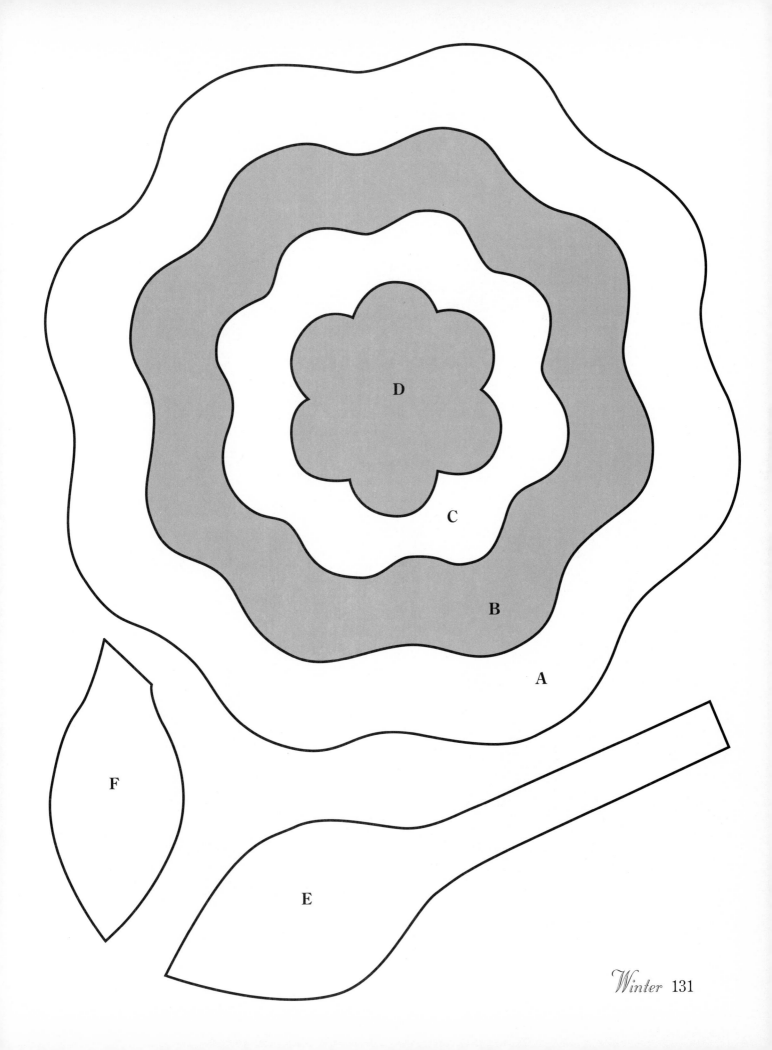

D

C

B

A

F

E

The cool beauty of February's birthstone is reflected in the colors of this charming patchwork pattern, also known as Diamond Star, Windmill, and Golden Wedding.

Amethyst

Finished Size
Blocks: 12 blocks, 18" square
Quilt: 73" x 91"

Materials
5 yards of pink/blue print fabric (includes binding)
2¼ yards of muslin for unpieced inner border (or 1 yard for pieced border)
1⅞ yards of ice blue print fabric
¾ yard of cranberry print fabric
5½ yards of backing fabric

Cutting
1. See page 145 for tips on making templates. Make templates for patterns A, B, and C.
2. Cut 48 As from cranberry print fabric.
3. Cut 192 Bs from ice blue fabric.
4. From pink/blue print fabric, cut 2 (6½" x 76") strips and 2 (6½" x 94") strips for borders. Set aside a 15" x 94" piece for straight-grain binding.
5. From remaining pink/blue print fabric, cut 192 Cs.
6. From muslin, cut 2 (4" x 81") strips and 2 (4" x 63") strips for unpieced inner borders. Or, to make pieced borders, cut 8 (4" x 42") crossgrain strips and piece them in pairs end-to-end to make border strips of needed lengths.

Piecing
1. Join B triangles to 2 opposite sides of each A square. Press seam allowances toward Bs. Join Bs to remaining sides of A squares.
2. Referring to Piecing diagram, set a C triangle into each opening between Bs.

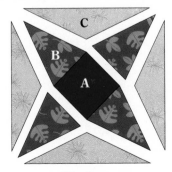

Piecing

3. Make 4 pieced squares for each block. Arrange squares as shown in Block Assembly diagram. For each block, join units in pairs. Press joining seam allowances in opposite directions. Join pairs. Make 12 blocks.

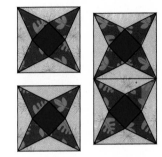

Block Assembly

Quilt Top Assembly
1. Referring to photograph, arrange blocks in 4 horizontal rows of 3 blocks each. Join blocks in each row. Join rows to assemble quilt top.
2. Mark centers on edges of each border strip. Matching centers, join 63" muslin strips and 76" print strips in pairs. Join long strips in same manner.
3. Mark centers on edges of quilt top. Matching centers of borders and quilt top, join shorter borders to top and bottom edges. Add long borders to sides in same manner. See page 151 for tips on mitering border corners.

Quilting and Finishing
Use purchased stencils to mark quilting designs in borders. Outline-quilt blocks; then quilt borders as marked.

See page 157 for instructions on making and applying straight-grain binding.

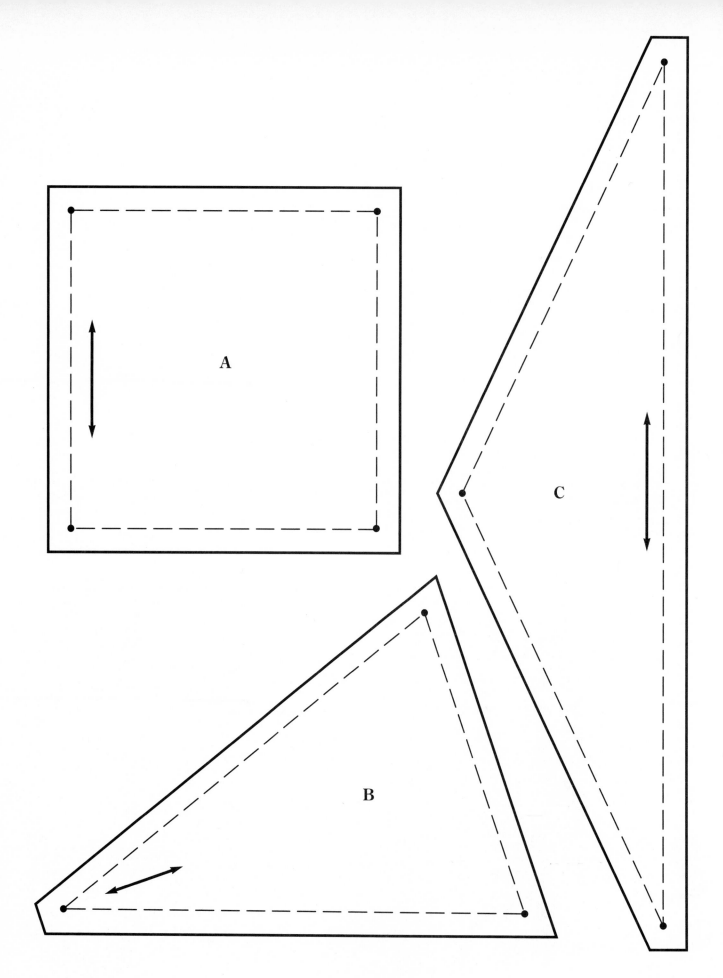

In the Bleak Midwinter

A haunting melody transforms Christina Rossetti's poem of winter chill into a favorite hymn. So can seemingly drab fabric scraps mix to make a beautiful quilt, proving even the easiest piecing creates dramatic results.

In the Bleak Midwinter

Finished Size
Blocks: 30 blocks, 11½" square
Quilt: 76½" x 88"

Materials
4 yards of light gray solid or miniprint fabric
2¼ yards of black print fabric for outer border
Scraps or ¼-yard pieces of 11 black/white print fabrics
1 yard of black solid fabric for binding
5¼ yards of backing fabric

Cutting
Note: Cutting instructions for patchwork pieces differ for traditional piecing and quick piecing. Cutting instructions for patchwork pieces are given with directions for each technique.

For borders, cut 4 (3½" x 72") strips of gray fabric and 4 (7" x 80") strips of black print fabric.

Traditional Piecing
1. See page 145 for tips on making templates. Make a template for Triangle A.

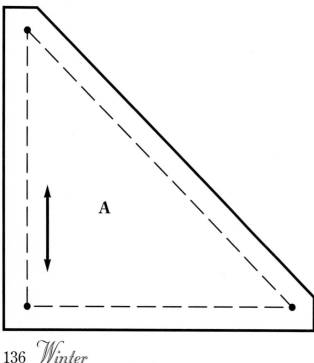

2. Cut 480 As from gray fabric.
3. Cut 40 As from each black print, including border fabric, to make 480 black As.
4. Join black and gray triangles, making 480 triangle-squares. Press all seam allowances toward black fabrics.
5. Join triangle-squares in pairs; then combine pairs to make a 4-square unit as shown in Piecing diagram.
6. Make 4 pieced units for each block. Arrange pieced units as shown in Block Assembly diagram. Join units in rows, pressing joining seam allowances in each row in opposite directions. Join rows to complete block. Make 30 blocks.

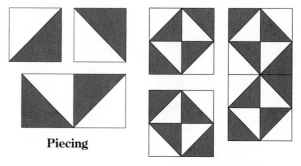

Piecing

Block Assembly

Quick Piecing
Note: This block is ideal for quick piecing short-cuts. See page 148 for detailed instructions on making quick-pieced triangle-squares.
1. Cut 24 (9" x 21") pieces of gray fabric.
2. From each black print (including border fabric), cut 2 (9" x 21") pieces.
3. On wrong side of each gray piece, mark a 2 x 5-square grid of 3¾" squares. Draw a diagonal line through each square as shown in Triangle-Square Grid diagram.

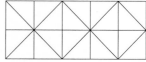

Triangle-Square Grid

4. Pin a gray rectangle to each black piece, with right sides facing. Following directions for half-square triangles on page 148, machine-stitch grids. Cut 20 triangle-squares from each grid. Press seam allowances toward black fabrics.
5. Follow steps 5 and 6 under Traditional Piecing to make 30 blocks.

Quilt Top Assembly
1. Referring to photograph, arrange blocks in 6 horizontal rows of 5 blocks each. Join blocks in each row. Join rows to assemble quilt top.
2. Mark centers on edges of each border strip. Matching centers, join gray and black strips in pairs.
3. Mark centers on edges of quilt top. Matching centers

of borders and quilt top, join borders to top and bottom edges. Add borders to sides in same manner. See page 151 for tips on mitering border corners.

Quilting and Finishing

Quilt each block as shown in Quilting diagram. Quilt borders as desired.

See page 157 for instructions on making and applying bias or straight-grain binding.

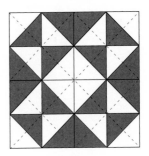

Quilting

Make this wintry-looking
lap quilt so you can
cuddle up with
someone you love for
Valentine's Day.
The warmth of love is a
reminder that spring is
only five weeks away.

Snowy, Snowy Night Lap Quilt

Finished Size
Block: 20 blocks, 12" x 13¾"
Quilt: 56½" x 77¼"

Materials
4 yards of white solid fabric (includes binding)
2 yards of slate blue minidot fabric
1 yard each of navy print and sky blue print fabrics
3½ yards of backing fabric (or 1¾ yards of 90"-wide sheeting)

Cutting
1. See page 145 for tips on making templates. Make templates of patterns A, B, and C.
2. From white fabric, cut 2 (4½" x 79") strips and 2 (4½" x 58") strips for borders. Cut and set aside a 12" x 79" piece of white fabric for binding.
3. For patchwork, cut 360 As each from navy and sky blue print fabrics.
4. From remaining white fabric, cut 260 Bs.
5. Cut 13 (2¼" x 42") crossgrain strips of slate blue minidot fabric. From these, cut 130 Cs, placing template grainline parallel to edges of each strip.
6. From remaining slate blue fabric, cut 128 Bs.

Piecing
The Snowflake blocks can be pieced in straight seams (that is, without having to set in) until the last row of the hexagonal block. Refer to block assembly diagrams (Figures 1–5) while assembling each block.
1. Begin the center unit of each block by sewing sky blue As to 3 sides of a white B (Figure 1). Press seam allowances toward blue fabric.
2. Join 3 sky blue As and 4 navy As in a row as shown in Figure 1. Join pieced row to bottom edge of center unit.
3. Join 3 sky blue As and 5 navy As in a row as shown in Figure 2. Join row to left side of center unit.
4. Join 3 sky blue As and 6 navy As in a row as shown in Figure 3. Join row to right side of center unit.
5. Join 2 sky blue As and 1 navy A as shown in Figure 4; then join a white B to each end of row as shown. Make 3 of these rows; then join 1 row to each side of center unit as shown.

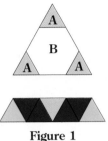
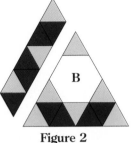

Figure 1　　**Figure 2**

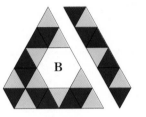

Figure 3

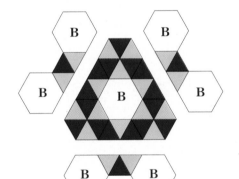

Figure 4

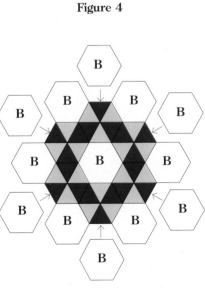

Figure 5

6. Set 6 white Bs into openings around each block as shown in Figure 5, referring to page 148 for tips on making set-in seams. Make 20 blocks, marking top of each block with a pin.

Quilt Top Assembly

1. Referring to Row Assembly diagram, join 5 blocks to make a vertical row as shown. (For clarity of illustration, this diagram shows only outer row of each block.) Set slate blue Bs into openings between blocks as shown. Make 4 vertical rows.

2. Select first row. Referring to Quilt Assembly diagram, set a C diamond into each opening on left side of row. Press seam allowances toward diamonds. When row is complete, use a rotary cutter with an acrylic ruler to trim jagged edges of diamonds as shown, leaving ¼"

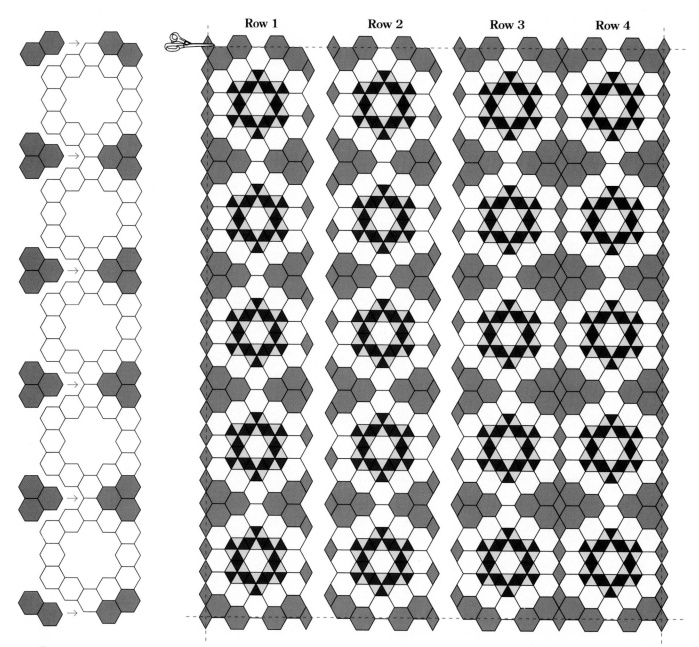

Row Assembly

Row 1   Row 2   Row 3   Row 4

Quilt Assembly

seam allowances beyond points of B hexagons.

3. On the right edge of first row, set a C diamond into every other opening as shown in Joining Rows diagram. Set diamonds in alternating openings on left edge of second row; then join rows as shown. (This zigzag path cuts in half the number of set-ins required in the seam that joins rows.)

4. Referring to Quilt Assembly diagram, join rows 3 and 4 in same manner.

5. Join Cs to right edge of fourth row in same manner as on first row. Trim jagged edge of diamonds as

Joining Rows

before. Trim top and bottom edges as shown in Quilt Assembly diagram.

6. Mark centers on edges of each white border strip. Mark centers on each edge of quilt top.

7. Matching centers of borders and quilt top, join borders to top and bottom edges. Add borders to quilt sides in same manner. See page 151 for tips on mitering border corners.

Quilting and Finishing

Outline-quilt patchwork. Quilt border as desired.

See page 157 for instructions on making and applying straight-grain binding.

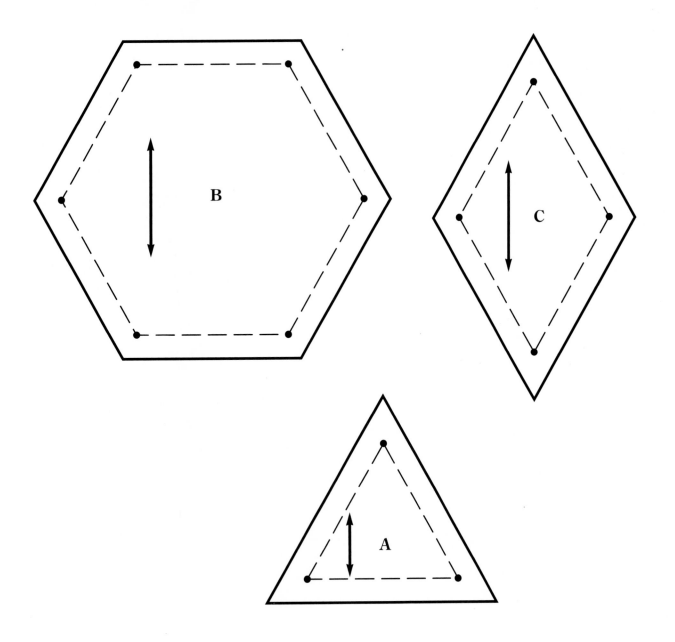

Workshop

Work that springs from the heart's desire,
Setting the brain and the soul on fire—
Oh, what is so good as the heat of it,
And what is so glad as the beat of it,
And what is so kind as the stern command,
Challenging brain and heart and hand?
Angela Morgan, "A Song of Triumph"

Like most forms of handwork, quiltmaking
evolves with passing generations, each era leaving its stamp. True to tradition, today's quilters
mix time-honored needle skills with clever new
tools and techniques that enhance creativity and
productivity. The following guide is a map of conventional quiltmaking methods, but remember—
you are free to find your own path.

the necessary length. Usually, other pieces can be cut aligned with either grain.

Bias is the 45° diagonal line between the two grain directions. Bias has the most stretch and is used for curving strips such as flower stems. Bias is often preferred for binding.

Never use the selvage (finished edge). Selvage does not react to washing, drying, and pressing like the rest of the fabric and may pucker when the finished quilt is laundered.

Scissors or Rotary Cutter?

Each cutting tool has advantages over the other. You'll always need trusty scissors, particularly for cutting curved and irregular shapes. But if you're not using a rotary cutter, you may be spending more time than necessary on cutting. Several quilts in this book are well suited for rotary cutting.

Rotary Cutting

A rotary cutter, used with a protective mat and a ruler, takes getting used to but is very efficient for cutting strips, squares, and triangles. A rotary cutter is fast because you can measure and cut multiple layers with a single stroke, without templates or marking. It is also more accurate than cutting with scissors because fabrics remain flat and unmoving during cutting.

Because the blade is very sharp, be sure to get a rotary cutter with a safety guard. Keep the guard in the safe position at all times, except when making a cut. Always keep the cutter out of the reach of children.

Use the cutter with a self-healing mat. A good mat for cutting strips is at least 23" wide.

1. Squaring the fabric is the first step in accurate cutting. Fold the fabric with selvages aligned. With the yardage to your right, align a small square ruler with the fold near the cut edge. Place a long ruler against the left side of the square (Diagram 6). Keeping the long ruler in place, remove the square. Hold the ruler in place with your left hand as you cut, rolling the cutter *away from you* along the ruler's edge with a steady motion. You can move your left hand along the ruler as you cut, but do not change the position of the ruler. *Keep your fingers away from the ruler's edge when cutting.*

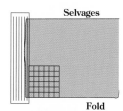
Diagram 6

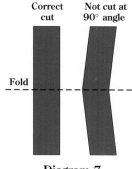
Diagram 7

2. Open the fabric. If the cut was not accurately perpendicular to the fold, the edge will be V-shaped instead of straight (Diagram 7). Correct the cut if necessary.

3. With a transparent ruler, you can measure and cut at the same time. Fold the fabric in half again, aligning the selvages with the fold, making four layers that line up perfectly along the cut edge. Project instructions designate the strip width needed. Position the ruler to measure the correct distance from the edge (Diagram 8) and cut. The blade will easily cut through all four layers. Check the strip to be sure the cut is straight. The strip length is the width of the fabric, approximately 43" to 44". Using the ruler again, trim selvages, cutting about ⅜" from each end.

4. To cut squares and rectangles from a strip, align the desired measurement on the ruler with the strip end and cut across the strip (Diagram 9).

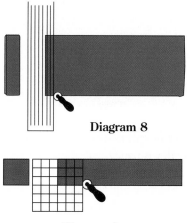
Diagram 8

Diagram 9

5. Cut triangles from squares or rectangles. Cutting instructions often direct you to cut a square in half or in quarters diagonally to make right triangles, and this technique can apply to rectangles, too (Diagram 10). The outside edges of the square are on the straight of the grain, so triangle sides cut on the diagonal are bias.

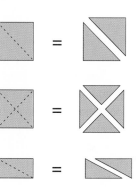
Diagram 10

6. Some projects in this book use a timesaving technique called strip piecing. With this method, strips are joined to make a pieced band. Cut across the seams of this band to cut preassembled units (Diagram 11).

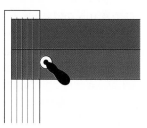
Diagram 11

7. You can rotary-cut bias strips. Square the edge and open the fabric to one layer. Bring the edge up to one selvage (Diagram 12), making a 45° angle along the fold. Trim ⅛" from the fold and then cut desired strips (Diagram 13). Bias stretches easily, so press down on the ruler when cutting to keep the fabric from shifting.

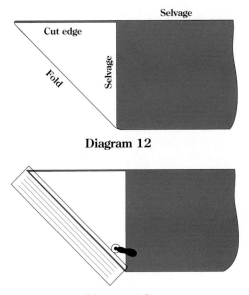

Diagram 12

Diagram 13

Cutting Strips with Scissors

Those who cut with scissors can also use strip piecing techniques. You need good shears, a gridded 24"-long acrylic ruler, and a small square ruler.

To mark cutting lines on fabric, refer to Rotary Cutting, Step 1 and Diagram 6, to mark a straight line from which to measure the strip. Remove the square, hold the ruler firmly in place, and draw a line against its edge. Start with this line to measure strip width.

To keep layers from shifting during cutting, pin between marked lines. Cut on each line with scissors, using a firm, steady motion. Sharp scissors should easily make a smooth cut through four layers.

Piecing

The right way to piece a quilt is the way that works best for you. You may find that machine piecing is best in one situation and hand piecing in another.

Examples of machine-sewn quilts date to soon after the invention of the sewing machine in 1846, so we know quiltmakers began using it right away. Machine stitching does not diminish the quality of a quilt, as evidenced by museum collections that include many fine quilts—old and new—stitched entirely by machine.

Machine Piecing

Your sewing machine does not have to be a new, computerized model. A good straight stitch is all that's necessary, but it may be helpful to have a nice satin stitch for appliqué. Clean and oil your machine regularly, use good-quality thread, and replace needles frequently.

1. Patches for machine piecing are cut with the seam allowance included, but the sewing line is not usually marked. Therefore, a way to make a consistent ¼" seam is essential. Some presser feet have a right toe that is ¼" from the needle. Other machines have an adjustable needle that can be set for a ¼" seam. If your machine has neither feature, experiment to find how the fabric must be placed to make a ¼" seam.

2. Use a stitch length that makes a strong seam but is not too difficult to remove with a seam ripper. The best setting is usually 10–12 stitches per inch.

3. Pin only when really necessary. If a straight seam is less than 4" and if it does not have to match an adjoining seam, pinning is not necessary.

4. When intersecting seams must align (Diagam 14), match the units with right sides facing and push a pin through both seams at the seam line. Turn the pinned unit to the right side to check the alignment; then pin securely. As you sew, remove each pin just before the needle reaches it.

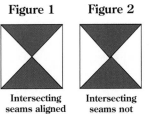

Figure 1   **Figure 2**

Intersecting seams aligned   Intersecting seams not aligned

Diagram 14

5. Block assembly diagrams are used throughout this book to show how pieces should be joined. Make small units first; then join them in rows and continue joining rows to finish the block (Diagram 15). Blocks are joined in the same manner to complete the quilt top.

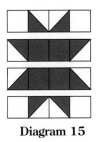

Diagram 15

6. Chain piecing saves time. Stack pieces to be sewn in pairs, with right sides facing. Join the first pair as usual. At the end of the seam, do not backstitch, cut the thread, or lift the presser foot. Just feed in the next pair of pieces—the machine will make a few stitches between pieces before the needle strikes the second piece of fabric. Continue sewing in this way until all pairs are joined. Stack the chain of pieces until you are ready to clip them apart (Diagram 16).

Diagram 16

7. Most seams are sewn straight across, from raw edge to raw edge. Since they will be crossed by other seams, they do not require backstitching to secure them.

8. When piecing diamonds or other angled seams, you may need to make set-in seams. For these, always mark the corner dots (shown on the patterns) on the fabric pieces. Stitch one side, starting at the outside edge and being careful not to sew past the dot into the seam allowance (Diagram 17, Figure 1). Backstitch. Align the other side of the piece as needed, with right sides facing. Sew from the dot to the outside edge (Figure 2).

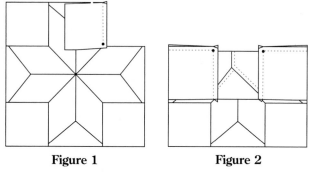

| Figure 1 | Figure 2 |

Diagram 17

9. Sewing curved seams requires extra care. First, mark the centers of both the convex (outward) and concave (inward) curves (Diagram 18). Staystitch just inside the seam allowance of both pieces. Clip the concave piece to the stitching (Figure 1). With right sides facing and raw edges aligned, pin the two patches together at the center (Figure 2) and at the left edge

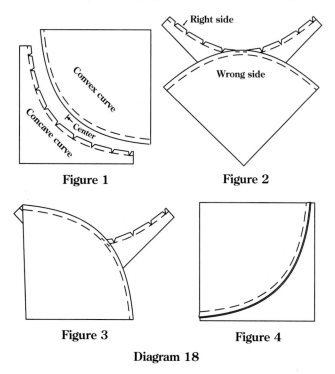

Figure 1   Figure 2

Figure 3   Figure 4

Diagram 18

(Figure 3). Sew from edge to center, stopping frequently to check that the raw edges are aligned. Stop at the center with the needle down. Raise the presser foot and pin the pieces together from the center to the right edge. Lower the foot and continue to sew. Press seam allowances toward the concave curve (Figure 4).

Hand Piecing

Make a running stitch of 8 to 10 stitches per inch along the marked seam line on the wrong side of the fabric. Don't pull the fabric as you sew; let the pieces lie relaxed in your hand. Sew from seam line to seam line, not from edge to edge as in machine piecing.

When ending a line of stitching, backstitch over the last stitch and make a loop knot (Diagram 19).

Match seams and points accurately, pinning patches together before piecing. Align match points as described in Step 4 under Machine Piecing.

Diagram 19

When joining units where several seams meet, do not sew over seam allowances; sew *through* them at the match point (Diagram 20). When four or more seams meet, press the seam allowances in the same direction to reduce the bulk (Diagram 21).

Diagram 20   **Diagram 21**

Pressing

Careful pressing is necessary for precise piecing. Press each seam as you go. Sliding the iron back and forth may push the seam out of shape. Use an up-and-down motion, lifting the iron from spot to spot. Press the seam flat on the wrong side. Open the piece and, on the right side, press both seam allowances to one side (usually toward the darker fabric). Pressing the seam open leaves tiny gaps through which batting may beard.

Quick-Pieced Triangles

Right triangles can be cut and sewn traditionally, but quick machine-piecing methods save time. By sewing on a large piece of marked fabric before any cutting is done, you can eliminate the labor of making a template, tracing it repeatedly on fabric, cutting out each triangle, and joining one pair at a time. With quick piecing, a few minutes of sewing result in a pile of ready-to-go and accurately pieced units. These techniques are most useful when making many sets of pieced triangles from the same two fabrics.

The technique for quick-pieced triangles involves marking a grid on the *wrong* side of the fabric and stitching diagonal lines through the grid. When the grid is cut apart, you'll have preassembled units. The size of the fabric piece needed for quick piecing is stated in the project instructions.

Half-Square Triangles

When two same-size right triangles are joined along diagonal edges to form a square, it is called a triangle-square. Each triangle equals half the square.

1. The project instructions illustrate and describe the grid, stating the number and size of the squares needed. These squares are ⅞" larger than the leg of the desired *finished* triangle. Draw diagonal lines through the grid as illustrated for the project (Diagram 22).

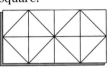

Diagram 22

2. Match the marked fabric to its companion fabric, with right sides facing. Pin the layers together along horizontal and vertical lines of the grid, avoiding diagonal lines so the pins will not interfere with stitching.
3. Machine-stitch exactly ¼" from *both* sides of all *diagonal* lines (Diagram 23). At corners, pivot the fabric without lifting the needle.

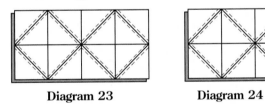

Diagram 23   **Diagram 24**

4. When stitching is done, trim the excess fabric around the grid; then cut on all horizontal and vertical grid lines, cutting the fabric into squares (Diagram 24).
5. Next, cut on the diagonal line between the stitching to separate the two triangle-squares (Diagram 25).

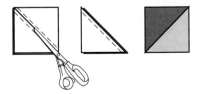

Diagram 25

6. Press seam allowances toward the darker fabric. Cut points off the seam allowances, making a neat square. Be careful not to pull on the seam, as this will stretch the bias and distort the square.

Quarter-Square Triangles

Another type of triangle-square is formed by joining the legs of four same-size right triangles. With a few differences, quarter-square triangles are joined in the same manner as half-square triangles.

1. Mark one fabric piece as illustrated in the project instructions. These squares are 1¼" larger than the hypotenuse of the desired *finished* triangle. Draw diagonal lines through the grid.
2. Match the marked fabric to its companion fabric, with right sides facing, and pin.
3. Machine-stitch ¼" from *both* sides of *only one diagonal line* in each square (Diagram 26).

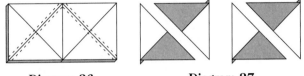

Diagram 26   **Diagram 27**

4. When stitching is done, trim the excess fabric around the grid. Cut on *all* marked grid lines, cutting the fabric into triangles. Press all seam allowances toward the darker fabric.
5. Join two of these pieced triangles to make a square (Diagram 27).

Appliqué

The word *appliqué* is French, meaning to apply (as a decoration) to a larger surface. In quiltmaking, appliqués are cut out and sewn to a background fabric. Since there are several appliqué techniques, test different methods to discover your favorite. The curves or points of the design may determine the method most suitable for a specific project.

Traditional Hand Appliqué

Hand appliqué requires that you turn under a seam allowance around the shape to prevent frayed edges.
1. See page 145 for tips on making templates for appliqué. Trace around the template on the right side of the fabric. This line indicates where to turn the seam allowance. Cut each piece approximately ¼" outside the line.
2. For simple shapes, turn the edges by pressing the seam allowance to the back; complex shapes may require basting the seam allowance. Sharp points and strong curves are best appliquéd with freezer paper (see page 150). Clip curves to make a smooth edge. With practice, you can work without pressing seam allowances, turning edges under with the needle as you sew.

3. Do not turn under any seam allowance that will be covered by another appliqué piece.

4. To stitch, use one strand of cotton-wrapped polyester sewing thread in a color that matches the appliqué. Use a slipstitch, but keep the stitch very small on the surface. Working from right to left, pull the needle through the base fabric and catch only a few threads on the folded edge of the appliqué. Reinsert the needle into the base fabric, under the top thread on the appliqué edge to keep the thread from tangling (Diagram 28).

5. An alternative to slipstitching is to work a decorative buttonhole stitch around each figure (Diagram 29).

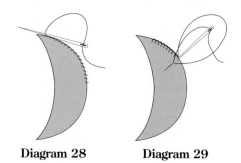

Diagram 28   Diagram 29

Freezer Paper Hand Appliqué

Supermarket freezer paper saves time because it eliminates the need for basting seam allowances.

1. Trace the template onto the *dull* side of the freezer paper and cut the paper on the marked line. *Note:* If a design is not symmetrical, turn the template over and trace a mirror image so the fabric piece won't be reversed when you cut it out.

2. Pin the freezer paper shape, with its *shiny side* up, to the *wrong side* of the fabric. Following the paper shape and adding a scant ¼" seam allowance, cut out the fabric piece. Do not remove pins.

3. Using just the tip of a dry iron, press the seam allowance to the shiny side of the paper. Be careful not to touch the freezer paper with the iron.

4. Appliqué the piece to the background as in traditional appliqué. Trim the fabric from behind the shape, leaving ¼" seam allowances. Separate the freezer paper from the fabric with your fingernail and pull gently to remove it. If you prefer not to trim the background fabric, pull out the freezer paper before you complete stitching.

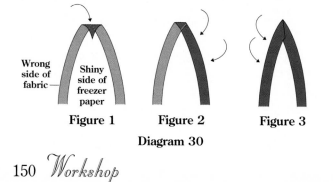

Wrong side of fabric   **Shiny side of freezer paper**

Figure 1   Figure 2   Figure 3

Diagram 30

5. Sharp points require special attention. Turn the point down and press it (Diagram 30, Figure 1). Fold the seam allowance on one side over the point and press it (Figure 2); then fold the other seam allowance over the point and press (Figure 3).

6. When pressing curved edges, clip sharp inward curves (Diagram 31). If the shape doesn't curve smoothly, separate the paper from the fabric with your fingernail, and try again.

Clip

Wrong side of fabric

Right side of fabric, pressed to freezer paper

Shiny side of freezer paper

Diagram 31

7. Remove the pins when all seam allowances have been pressed to the freezer paper. Position the prepared appliqué right side up on the background fabric. Press to adhere it to the background fabric.

Faced Appliqué

For complex shapes or hard-to-handle fabrics, try facing the appliqué piece. Cut the shape from the appliqué fabric; then cut an identical piece from batiste or a similar lightweight fabric. Join the pieces along the marked seam line. Clip seam allowances at points and curves. Cut a small slit in the lining (Diagram 32), turn the unit right side out through the slit, and press. The edges will be neatly turned and the piece is ready to be appliquéd.

Diagram 32

Machine Appliqué

A machine-sewn satin stitch makes a neat edging. For machine appliqué, cut appliqué pieces without adding seam allowances.

Using fusible web to adhere pieces to the background adds a stiff extra layer to the appliqué and is not appropriate for some quilts. It is best used on small pieces, difficult fabrics, or for wall hangings and accessories in which added stiffness is acceptable. The web prevents fraying and shifting during appliqué.

Place tear-away stabilizer under the background fabric behind the appliqué. Machine-stitch the appliqué edges with a satin stitch or close-spaced zigzag (Diagram 33). Test stitch length and width on a sample first. Use an open-toed presser foot. Remove the stabilizer when appliqué is complete.

Diagram 33

Embroidery Stitches

Running Stitch
Make stitches, leaving even, stitch-length spaces between them.

Satin Stitch
Bring the needle up on one side of the design and make a stitch to the opposite side. Slide the needle under the fabric and repeat, keeping stitches close and flat.

Figure 1

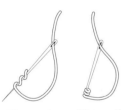

Figure 2

Chainstitch
Bring the thread up and make a loop (Figure 1). Holding the loop close to the fabric with your free thumb, insert the needle again as close as possible to where the thread first emerged. Bring the needle out a short distance away to start the next stitch. Do not pull the loops tight (Figure 2).

Lazy Daisy Stitch
Make a daisylike circle of single chainstitches, adding a small stitch at the end of each loop.

French Knot
Bring the needle up where the knot is to be. Holding the thread in your free hand, wrap it twice around the point of the needle (Figure 1). Holding the loops in place with your free hand, reinsert the needle as close as possible to where the thread first emerged (Figure 2).

Figure 1   **Figure 2**

Figure 3

Pull the needle through the loops to the wrong side of the fabric, forming a small round stitch (Figure 3).

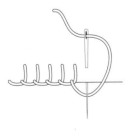

Blanket Stitch
Working from left to right, bring the needle up at the bottom of the design. Insert the needle above and to the right of this point. Keeping the thread behind the needle point, bring the needle out at the edge of the design.

Borders

Project instructions specify whether border corners should be straight or mitered. In all cases, measurements given for border strips include seam allowances and are slightly longer than necessary to allow for piecing variances. Borders are usually cut from the lengthwise grain before any other pieces are cut.

Measure First
Because seams may vary and some fabrics may stretch a bit, opposite sides of your assembled quilt top may not be the same measurement. You can (and should) correct this when you add borders.

Measure the length of each side of the quilt. Trim the side border strips to match the *shorter* of the two sides. Join borders to the quilt as described below, easing the longer side of the quilt to fit the border. Join borders to the top and bottom edges in the same manner.

Straight Borders
Side borders are usually added first (Diagram 34). With right sides facing and raw edges aligned, pin the center of one border strip to the center of one side of the quilt top. Pin the border to the quilt at each end and then pin along the side as desired. Machine-stitch with the border strip on top. Press the seam allowance toward the border. Trim excess border fabric at each end. In the same manner, add the border to the opposite side and then the top and bottom borders (Diagram 35).

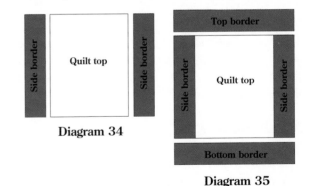

Diagram 34

Diagram 35

Mitered Borders
1. Measure your quilt sides. Trim side border strips to fit the shorter side *plus* the width of the border *plus* 2".
2. Center the measurement of the shorter side on one border strip, placing a pin at each end of the measurement and at the center.
3. With right sides facing and raw edges aligned, match the pins on the border strip to the center and corners of the longer side of the quilt. (Border fabric will extend beyond the corners.)

4. Start machine-stitching at the top pin, backstitching to lock the stitches. Continue to sew, easing the quilt between pins. Stop at the last pin and backstitch. Join remaining borders in the same manner. Press seam allowances toward borders.

5. With right sides facing, fold the quilt diagonally, aligning the raw edges of adjacent borders. Pin securely (Diagram 36).

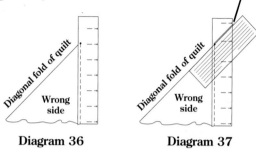

Diagram 36   **Diagram 37**

6. Align a yardstick or quilter's ruler along the diagonal fold (Diagram 37). Holding the ruler firmly, mark a line from the end of the border seam to the raw edge.

7. Start machine-stitching at the beginning of the marked line, backstitch, and then stitch on the line out to the raw edge.

8. Unfold the quilt to be sure that the corner lies flat. Correct the stitching if necessary. Trim the seam allowance to ¼".

9. Miter the remaining corners in the same manner. Press the corner seams open.

Marking Quilting Designs

Few subjects create as much discussion among quilters as how to mark a quilt top. Choosing a design that complements the quilt top is very important. The marks must stay on the top long enough for you to follow when quilting, but they must also be easily removed.

Choosing a Design

To find quilting patterns, begin by considering classic designs and traditional ways quilters have marked their quilts. For example, our grandmothers traced around plates or teacups to make circles for quilting. By tying a string to a pencil, quilters have traditionally made an oversized compass for marking graduated arcs. Overlapping squares and diamonds, too, have exciting possibilities. Traditional designs such as swags, feathers, cables, birds, and hearts are available as precut stencils.

Choose your quilting lines with care. The hours you spend connecting the layers of your quilt will create shadows and depths that magically bring your work to life. Make your lines count!

Quilting Without Marking

Some quilts can be quilted in-the-ditch (right along the seam line), outline-quilted (¼" from the seam line), or echo-quilted (lines of quilting rippling outward from the design like waves on a pond). These methods can be used without any marking at all. If you are machine quilting, simply use the edge of your presser foot and the seam line as a guide. If you are hand quilting, by the time you have pieced a quilt top, your eye will be practiced enough for you to produce straight, even quilting without the guidance of marked lines.

Another method that leaves no marks on the fabric is needle scratching. Use your quilting needle or a plastic tool called a **Hera Marker** to lightly scratch a line directly on the fabric. This technique works best on frame- or hoop-mounted work and only on 100% cotton fabrics. Needle marks will not show on fabrics with polyester content. Mark only a small area at a time (usually 4" or less) because the marks disappear quickly as you handle the quilt.

For straight-line quilting, try using narrow tape to mark the quilting lines. Do not use masking tape for this purpose, as the adhesive may leave a sticky residue on the quilt and may cause severe bearding in quilts with polyester batting. A better choice is a tape with a less sticky adhesive, such as **drafting tape** (available in graphic art or office supply stores) or **removable transparent tape** (sold under brand names such as Sewer's Fix-It Tape and 3-M Removable Magic Tape).

Marking Tools

Many quilters like to mark the entire top at one time, a practice that requires long-lasting markings. The most common tool for this purpose is a sharp **pencil**. However, most pencils are made with an oil-based graphite lead, which often will not wash out completely. Look for a high-quality artist's pencil marked "2H" or higher (the higher the number, the harder the lead, and the lighter the line it will make). Sharpen the pencil frequently to keep the line on the fabric thin and light. Or try a mechanical pencil with a 0.5-mm lead. It will maintain a fine line without sharpening.

While you are in the art supply store, get a **white plastic eraser** (brand name Magic Rub). This eraser, used by professional drafters and artists, will cleanly remove the carbon smudges left by pencil lead without fraying the fabric or leaving eraser crumbs.

Water- and **air-soluble marking pens** are convenient, but controversial, marking tools. Some quilters have found that the marks reappear, often up to several years later, while others have no problems with them.

Be sure to test these pens on each fabric you plan to mark and *follow package directions exactly.* Because the inks can be permanently set by heat, be very careful with a marked quilt. Do not leave it in your car on a hot day and never touch it with an iron until the marks have been removed. Plan to complete the quilting within a year after marking it with a water-soluble pen.

Air-soluble pens are best for marking small sections at a time. The marks disappear within 24 to 48 hours, but the ink remains in the fabric until it is washed. After the quilt is completed and before it is used, rinse it twice in clear, cool water, using no soap, detergent, or bleach. Let the quilt air-dry.

For dark fabrics, the cleanest marker you can use is a thin sliver of pure, white **soap.** Choose a soap that contains no creams, deodorants, dyes, or perfumes; these added ingredients may leave a residue on the fabric.

Other marking tools include **colored pencils** made specifically for marking fabric and **tailor's chalk** (available in powdered, stick, and traditional cake form). When using chalk, mark small sections of the quilt at a time because the chalk rubs off easily.

Making and Using Quilting Stencils

Quilting patterns can be purchased as precut stencils. Simply lay these on your quilt top and mark the design through the cutout areas.

To make your own stencil of a printed quilting pattern, use a permanent marker to trace the design onto template plastic. Then use a craft knife to cut out the design.

Another option is to use nylon tulle (the fine net used for bridal veils). Trace the design onto the tulle with a permanent marker. Then pin or tape the tulle onto the quilt top and retrace the design through the net with one of the marking tools discussed earlier.

Tracing Quilting Designs

If your quilt top is of light-colored fabrics, you may be able to trace the design directly onto the fabric. First trace the quilting design onto a sheet of white paper, using a *permanent* black marker. It is often a good idea to include alignment points on the drawing such as block corners or border widths to aid in positioning the quilt top properly.

When the ink is completely dry, tape the paper to a large, flat work surface. Place the quilt top over the paper, using alignment points to keep it straight and centered; then trace the design through the fabric.

If the fabric is too heavy or too dark to see through, put a light source under the design. If you do not have a light box, make your own by replacing the leaves of a table with a panel of glass; then set a lamp on the floor underneath the glass. Or tape the traced design to a window or glass door and fasten the quilt over it.

Batting

After you've marked your finished quilt top and are ready to quilt, you need to decide what kind of batting to use. The chart on page 154 identifies some characteristics of different brands.

Cotton Batting

Cotton batting is thin, so hand-quilting can be very fine. Manufacturers recommend quilting all-cotton batting closely, at intervals of ¼" to ½". However, manufacturers claim that the new needlepunched cotton batts can be quilted at greater intervals—from 2" to 10", depending on the brand.

Unlike polyester, cotton fibers do not beard (migrate through the fabric), making cotton a good choice for dark fabrics where loose fibers will be noticeable. Cotton will shrink about 5% when washed, which results in the wrinkled look characteristic of antique quilts.

At least one manufacturer now makes a blended batt of 80% cotton, with a polyester core. Cotton/polyester batts share the advantages of all-cotton—low loft, little or no bearding, wrinkling when washed—with the firm body and durability of polyester. They may be quilted at greater intervals (3" to 4") than cotton and should be preshrunk prior to quilting if you do not want wrinkles.

Polyester Batting

Polyester batting is available in a variety of thicknesses, from low loft to extremely high loft. Unlike cotton (which can be lumpy), polyester batting is uniform throughout the batt. It can be quilted at greater intervals than cotton without problems. It is durable and may be machine-washed without shrinking, making it the batting of choice for tailored quilts, puffy comforters, and other items which will be cleaned often.

Most polyester batts are bonded, glazed, or needle-punched to hold the fibers in place during quilting and to control bearding. However, all polyester batts will beard to some extent, except Thermore.

Needlepunched fibers tend to migrate greatly at first, with bearding tapering off as the quilt is washed repeatedly. Bonded and glazed batts behave in the opposite manner—bearding increases over time as repeated washing dissolves the resin.

Bearding is most visible on dark fabrics. One manufacturer addresses the problem with Polydown DK, a dark gray, medium-loft bonded batting. Although these fibers will migrate to the surface of the quilt over time, they will be less visible against dark fabrics.

Thermore, developed for use in quilted clothing, has hollow fibers unlike those in other polyester batts. Thermore has been tested by the manufacturer through 300 wash cycles with no perceptible bearding.

Wool Batting

The advantage of wool batting is the ease of quilting—it's like stitching through butter. But wool beards and requires extra care to wash. Quilts with wool batting should be hand-washed in cold water. A wool quilt is very heavy when wet, so it should be towel-squeezed as much as possible and left stretched out flat to air-dry.

Batting Comparison Chart

	FIBER	LOFT	FINISH	SIZES AVAILABLE				
				Crib 45" x 60"	Twin 72" x 90"	Full 81" x 96"	Queen 90" x 108"	King 120" x 120"
MOUNTAIN MIST								
Bleached Cotton	Cotton	Low	Glazed	-	-	x	x*	-
Blue Ribbon Cotton	Cotton	Very Low	Punched	x	-	-	x	-
Polyester	Polyester	Medium	Glazed	x	x	x	x	x
Quilt-Light	Polyester	Low	Glazed	x	-	x	x	-
Fatt Batt	Polyester	High	Glazed	x	x	x	x	-
HOBBS								
Polydown	Polyester	Medium	Bonded	x	-	x	x	x
Polydown DK	Polyester	Medium	Bonded	-	-	-	x	-
Thermore	Polyester	Low	Bonded	-	-	-	x**	-
Heirloom	Cotton	Low	Punched	-	-	-	x	-
Cloud Lite	Polyester	Low	Bonded	x	x	x	x	x
Cloud Loft	Polyester	High	Bonded	x	-	x	x	x
FAIRFIELD Poly-Fil								
Traditional	Polyester	Medium	Punched	x	x	x	x	x
Extra-Loft	Polyester	High	Bonded	x	x	x	x	x
Ultra-Loft	Polyester	High	Punched	x	x	x	x	-
Low-Loft	Polyester	Low	Bonded	x	-	x	x	x
Hi-Loft	Polyester	High	Bonded	x	-	-	x	-
Cotton Classic	Cotton/ Polyester	Low	Bonded	-	-	x	-	-
CRAFTER'S CABIN	Polyester	Medium	Bonded	x	-	x	x	x
WARM & NATURAL	Cotton	Low	Punched	-	-	-	x	-

*81" x 108"   **Also available in 27" x 45", 54" x 45", and 45"-wide rolls

Making a Quilt Backing

Some fabric and quilt shops sell 90" and 108" widths of 100% cotton sheeting that are very practical for quilt backing. However, the instructions in this book always give backing yardage based on 44"-wide fabric.

When using 44"-wide fabric, all quilts wider than 41" will require a pieced backing. For quilts 42"–80" wide, you will need an amount of fabric equal to two times the desired *length* of the unfinished backing. (The unfinished backing should be at least 3" larger on all sides than the quilt top.)

The simplest method of making a backing is to cut the fabric in half widthwise (Diagram 38), and then sew the two panels together lengthwise. This results in a backing with a vertical center seam. Press the seam allowances to one side.

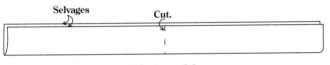

Diagram 38

Another method of seaming the backing results in two vertical seams and a center panel of fabric. This method is often preferred by quilt show judges. Begin by cutting the fabric in half widthwise. Open the two lengths and stack them, with right sides facing and selvages aligned. Stitch along *both* selvage edges to create a tube of fabric (Diagram 39). Cut down the center of the top layer of fabric only and open the fabric flat (Diagram 40). Press seam allowances to one side.

Diagram 39

If the quilt is wider than 80", it is more economical to cut the fabric into three lengths that are the desired width of the backing. Join the three lengths so that the seams are horizontal to the quilt, rather than vertical. For this method, you'll need

Diagram 40

an amount of fabric equal to three times the *width* of the unfinished backing.

Fabric requirements in this book reflect the most economical method of seaming the backing fabric.

Layering and Basting

After the quilt top and backing are made, the next steps are layering and basting in preparation for quilting.

Prepare a large working surface to spread out the quilt—a large table, two tables pushed together, or the floor. Place the backing on the working surface wrong side up. Unfold the batting and place it on top of the backing, smoothing away any wrinkles or lumps.

Lay the quilt top wrong side down on top of the batting and backing. Make sure edges of the backing and quilt top are parallel (Diagram 41).

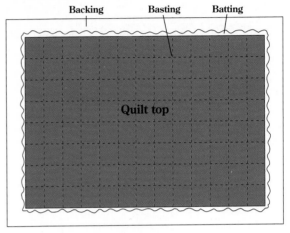

Diagram 41

Knot a long strand of sewing thread and use a long (darning) needle for basting. Begin basting in the center of the quilt and baste out toward the edges. The basting stitches should cover an ample amount of the quilt so that the layers do not shift during quilting.

Machine quilters use nickel-plated safety pins for basting so there will be no basting threads to get caught on the presser foot. Safety pins, spaced approximately 4" apart, can be used by hand quilters, too.

The Quilting Stitch

Quilting is the process of stitching the three layers of a quilt together, by hand or by machine, usually using a straight or running stitch. Consider the design, intended use, and your personal preference to decide whether to quilt a project by hand or by machine.

Hand Quilting
Hand-quilted stitches should be evenly spaced, with the spaces between stitches about the same length as the stitches themselves. The *number* of stitches per inch is

less important than the *uniformity* of the stitching. Don't worry if you take only five or six stitches per inch; just be consistent throughout the project.

1. Start by placing your work in a frame or a hoop. Sit in a comfortable chair near good light. Have your thimble, scissors, thread, and quilting needles at hand. Position yourself so that the line of quilting angles from upper right to lower left, so that you can quilt toward yourself. (Reverse directions if you are left-handed.)

2. To quilt, use a short needle called a "between." Betweens come in sizes 7 to 12, with 7 being the longest and 12 the shortest. If you are a beginner, try a size 7 or 8; because betweens are so much shorter than other sewing needles, they may feel awkward at first. As your skill increases, a smaller needle will help you make smaller stitches.

3. To keep your thread from snarling and knotting as you stitch, thread the needle *before* you cut the thread from the spool. Cut an 18" to 24" length and make a small knot in the cut end.

4. Insert the needle from the top of the quilt, about 1" from the beginning of the quilting line. Slide the needle through the batting, but do not pierce the backing. Bring the needle up at the beginning point and gently pull the thread; the knot will stop on the surface. Tug the thread gently to pop the knot through the top into the batting. If it does not slip through, use the needle to gently separate the fabric threads and then tug again.

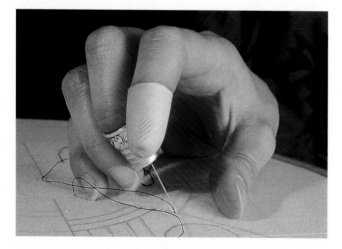

5. With your non-sewing hand under the quilt, insert the needle with the point straight down as shown in the photograph above, about ¹⁄₁₆" from the start. With your underneath finger, feel for the point as the needle comes through the backing. With practice, you will be able to find the point without pricking your finger.

6. Push the fabric up from below as you rock the needle to a nearly horizontal position. Using the thumb of

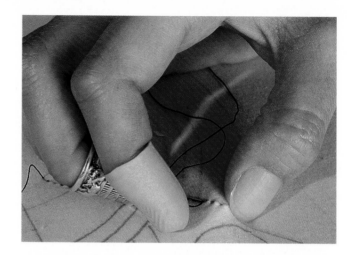

your sewing hand and the underneath hand as shown in the photograph above, pinch a little hill in the fabric and push the tip of the needle back through the quilt top.

7. Push the needle through to complete one stitch or rock the needle to an upright position to take another stitch before pulling it through. At first, load only two or three stitches on the needle. As you gain experience, try more stitches at one time, but take no more than a quarter-needleful before pulling the needle through. (Well-known quilter Ami Simms, shown in these photographs, uses a fingertip from a rubber glove on her index finger to provide traction for pulling the needle through.)

8. End the thread when you have 6" left. Tie a knot in the thread close to the quilt surface (Diagram 42). Pop the knot through the top as before (Diagram 43), and clip the tail. Rethread the needle and continue quilting.

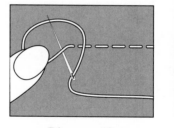 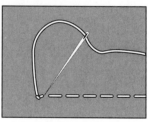

| Diagram 42 | Diagram 43 |

Machine Quilting

For machine quilting, the backing and batting should be 4" larger all around than the quilt top, because the quilting process pushes the quilt top fabric outward. After quilting, trim the backing and batting to the same size as the quilt top.

Thread your bobbin with good-quality sewing thread (not quilting thread) in a color to match the backing. Use a top thread color to match the quilt top or use invisible nylon thread.

An even-feed or walking foot will feed all the quilt's layers through the machine at the same speed. It is possible to machine-quilt without this foot (by experimenting with tension and presser foot pressure), but it will be much easier *with* it. If you do not have this foot, get one from your sewing machine dealer.

1. Roll both sides of the quilt toward the center. Leave a center section open, securing the rolled sides with bicycle clips (Diagram 44). These metal bands are sold in quilt shops and fabric stores.

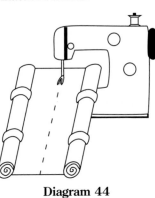

Diagram 44

2. Start stitching at the top center. Begin by stitching in place several times to lock the stitches.

3. Straight-line quilting is the easiest form of machine quilting. The seam lines for blocks and sashing form a grid across the length and width of the quilt. These are the longest lines of quilting, and they should be done first. Quilt down the center, from edge to edge.

4. Begin the next row at the bottom. Alternating the direction of quilting lines will keep the layers from shifting. Continue quilting half of the quilt, unrolling it until you reach the edge.

5. Remove the quilt from the machine and reroll the completed side. Turn the quilt and work out from the center again to complete the quilting on the other side.

6. When you have completed the vertical quilting lines, reroll the quilt in the other direction to quilt the horizontal lines in the same manner.

7. Some projects do not have vertical and horizontal quilting lines. Instead, the lines may be diagonal or follow the design of the patchwork. Always machine-quilt the longest lines first, starting in the center.

Tying Quilts

Tying is the fastest way to secure the three quilt layers. It is the only way to work with the thick batting that is often used for comforters. Colorful ties can also add a decorative effect to the overall design of your project.

Ties can be pearl cotton, yarn, ribbon floss, or narrow ribbon. The material used for ties should be strong enough to be tied very tightly and stay tied. Ties may be double knots, bows, pom-poms, or knots that hold buttons, charms, or beads. *Never use buttons or other small objects on quilts for babies or small children.*

Ties should be placed at least every 6". You will need a sharp embroidery needle with an eye large enough to

accommodate the tie material that you have chosen. Thread the needle but do not knot the thread end. Starting in the center of your basted quilt top, take a ⅛" to ¼" stitch through all three layers. Clip the thread, leaving a tail of thread several inches long on each side of the stitch (Diagram 45). Tie the two tails in a tight double knot (Diagram 46). Trim the tails of all the knots to the same length.

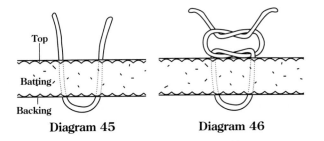

Diagram 45   **Diagram 46**

If you want to tie bows, leave longer tails and tie the double knot first; then tie the tails in a bow. Now tie the loops of the bow in a knot to be sure that the knot is very secure.

Wide ribbon is too difficult to pull through all three layers, but wide ribbon bows can look as if they are tied. Tie bows from 12" lengths of ribbon. With sewing thread that matches the ribbon color, hand-sew the bows in place, stitching through all three layers.

Binding

We recommend a double-layer binding, sometimes called French-fold binding. Double-layer binding wears well and is quick to apply. Instructions in this book allow for 2"-wide strips, which will yield a ⅜"-wide finished binding. If you use thick batting or if you prefer a wider binding, buy enough fabric to allow you to cut 3"-wide strips for a ⅝"-wide finished binding.

Straight-Grain Binding

1. Mark the fabric in horizontal lines the width of the binding (Diagram 47).

A	↕ 2"	
B		A
C		B
D		C
E		D
F		E
		F

Diagram 47

2. With right sides facing, fold the fabric in half, offsetting drawn lines by matching letters and raw edges (Diagram 48). Stitch a ¼" seam.

3. Cut the binding in a continuous strip, starting with one end and following the marked lines around the tube. Press the strip in half lengthwise.

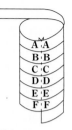

Diagram 48

Continuous Bias Binding

This technique can be used to make continuous bias for appliqué as well as for binding.

1. Cut a square of fabric in half diagonally to form two triangles. With right sides facing, join the triangles (Diagram 49). Press the seam allowance open.

2. Mark parallel lines the desired width of the binding (Diagram 50), taking care not to stretch the bias. With right sides facing, align the raw edges (indicated as Seam 2). As you align the edges, offset one Seam 2 point past its natural matching point by one line. Stitch the seam; then press the seam allowance open.

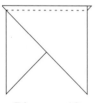

Diagram 49

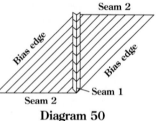

Diagram 50

3. Cut the binding in a continuous strip, starting with the protruding point and following the marked lines around the tube (Diagram 51). Press the strip in half lengthwise.

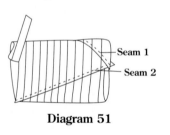

Diagram 51

Applying Binding

Binding is applied to the front of the quilt first. Begin anywhere on the edge of the quilt except at the corner.

1. Matching raw edges, lay the binding on the quilt. Fold down the top corner of the binding at a 45° angle, align the raw edges, and pin (Diagram 52).

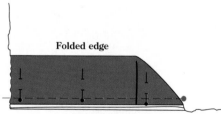

Folded edge

Diagram 52

2. Beginning at the folded end, machine-stitch the binding to the quilt. Stop stitching ¼" from the corner and backstitch. Fold the binding strip diagonally away from the quilt, making a 45° angle (Diagram 53).

3. Fold the binding strip straight down along the next side to be stitched, creating a pleat in the corner. Position the needle at the ¼" seam line of the new side (Diagram 54). Make a few stitches, backstitch, and then stitch the seam. Continue until all corners and sides are done. Overlap the end of the binding strip over the beginning fold and stitch about 2" beyond it. Trim any excess binding.

Front of quilt

Diagram 53

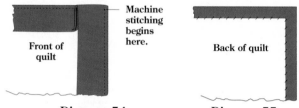

Diagram 54   **Diagram 55**

4. Turn the binding over the raw edge of the quilt. Slipstitch it in place on the back, using thread that matches the binding. The fold at the beginning of the binding makes a neat, angled edge when it is folded to the back.

5. At each corner, fold the binding to form a miter (Diagram 55). Hand-stitch the miters closed if desired.

Hanging Sleeve

Quilts that are hung for display should have a sleeve sewn to the back. A dowel or curtain rod, slipped through the sleeve, can hang from brackets on the wall.

1. Cut a 6"-wide fabric piece that measures the width of the quilt plus 2". Turn under ¼" hem on each end and press; then turn under 1" more. Press and topstitch.

2. With wrong sides facing, join long edges. Press the seam allowances open, centering the seam on one side of the tube. With the seam facing the quilt backing, place the sleeve just below the binding at the top of the quilt, centering it between the quilt sides (Diagram 56).

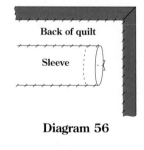

Back of quilt

Sleeve

Diagram 56

3. Slipstitch the top and bottom edges of the sleeve to the quilt backing only, making sure no stitches go through to the quilt top.

Glossary

Appliqué. Fabric pieces sewn to a foundation of fabric, usually applied by turning raw edges under and securing them with a hidden slipstitch. A close-set, machine zigzag (satin) stitch over raw edges may also be used.

Backing. The bottom fabric layer of a quilt.

Basting. A temporary running stitch used to secure fabrics prior to stitching.

Batting. The filler or middle of a quilt. Polyester batting is most widely used today and is available in various weights and thicknesses.

Bearding. The migration of batting fibers through the fabric to the quilt top.

Binding. Strips of fabric used to finish the raw edges around the perimeter of the quilt.

Block. A unit of patchwork, usually a square, repeated to make an entire quilt top.

Borders. One or more panels of fabric added to the outside edges of the quilt.

Cross-hatching. Quilting designs formed by grids of intersecting parallel lines.

Fat quarter. An 18" x 22" quarter-yard of fabric, made by cutting ½ yard in half widthwise.

Finger-pressing. Using your fingers or a fingernail to flatten or make a crease in fabric.

Fusible web. A material made of fibers that melt when heat is applied; used for fusing layers of fabric together.

Grain. The direction of woven threads in the fabric. Lengthwise threads run parallel to the selvage, and crosswise threads are perpendicular to the selvage.

Half-square triangles. Two equal right-angle triangles, joined to form a square.

In-the-ditch. Quilting worked in the seam or just beside the seam on the side without seam allowances.

Marking. The process of transferring designs onto the quilt top in order to have a line to follow when quilting.

Miter. A diagonal seam that forms a 45° angle at the meeting of two borders.

Outline quilting. Quilting stitched ¼" from the seam line to avoid seam allowances. You may have two stitching lines, ½" apart, flanking a seam line.

Piecing. The process of joining two or more pieces of fabric to form a design. Piecing can be done by hand or on the sewing machine with a regular-length stitch, coordinating thread, and a ¼" seam allowance.

Prairie points. Squares of fabric that are folded into triangles. They can be sewn into any seam but are usually sewn to the edge of a quilt as a decorative finish.

Quarter-square triangles. Four equal right-angle triangles, joined to form a square.

Quilt. A bed cover comprised of three layers: a decorative top, the filler or batting, and a backing. These layers are secured with running stitches (quilting) or with ties of yarn or pearl cotton.

Rotary cutter. A round-bladed cutting tool, used with a protective mat and acrylic ruler.

Sashing. Fabric strips that frame and separate the blocks of a quilt top.

Stencil. A template used for transferring a quilting design to the quilt top to provide a guide for quilting.

Strip set. A unit of joined strips which is cut into segments and then combined with others in a pieced design.

Tear-away stabilizer. A lightweight material used to keep fabric from shifting during machine appliqué.

Template. A reproduction of a pattern made from sturdy material.

Toile or toile de Jouy. A scenic pattern usually printed on fabric in one color on a light background, first popularized in 18th-century France.

Triangle-squares. Any pieced square made by joining equal right triangles.

Anatomy of a Quilt

The following diagrams of a quilt top and a quilt cross-section identify the different parts of a quilt as they are referred to in this book.

Acknowledgments

Irish Crosses, page 9: designed by Susan Ramey Wright; made by Annie C. Phillips.

Butterfly Crib Quilt, pages 11 and 13: designed and made by Patricia Ramey Channell.

Hosanna, page 15: designed and made by Joanne Cage.

Card Tricks, page 18: designed and made by Susan Ramey Wright.

Noah's Star Crib Quilt, page 21: designed and made by Carol M. Tipton.

Dutch Treat, page 31: designed by Susan Ramey Wright; made by Debra Steinman.

Dutch Treat Vest, page 33: designed and made by Cynthia Moody Wheeler.

Garden of Friendship, page 34: owned by Karen Veldboom; pieced by her grandmother, Henrietta Kroening; assembled and quilted by Mattie Borntreger.

Iris in My Garden, pages 6 and 39: designed and made by Zelda Wheeler Fasciano.

Windblown Girl, pages 43 and 44: designed and made by Zelda Wheeler Fasciano.

Wedding Ring, page 49: designed and made by Mary Ramey.

Sailboat Crib Quilt, page 51: designed and made by Joanne Cage.

Seven Sisters Quilt and Pillow, page 52: designed by Susan Ramey Wright; made by Judy Cantwell.

Paper Fans, pages 56 and 58: designed and made by Susan Ramey Wright.

Rose Garden, page 60: designed by Susan Ramey Wright; made by Annie C. Phillips.

Gone Fishin', page 46 and 65: designed by Susan Ramey Wright; made by Radine Robinson. Beach umbrella from Casual & Custom Furniture, Birmingham, Alabama.

Gone Fishin' Tote, pages 65 and 68: designed and made by Cynthia Moody Wheeler.

Turtle Creek, page 70: designed by Susan Ramey Wright; made by Carol M. Tipton.

Indian Summer, page 76: designed and made by Susan Ramey Wright.

Wild Goose Chase, page 79: designed and made by Susan Ramey Wright.

Spider Web, page 87: designed and pieced by Susan Ramey Wright; quilted by Annie C. Phillips.

Halloween Treat Bags, page 90: designed and made by Cynthia Moody Wheeler.

Maple Leaf, page 91: owned by Julia Roy.

Maple Leaf Pot Holders, page 93: designed and made by Cynthia Moody Wheeler.

Winds of Autumn, cover and page 94: designed and made by Barbara Bryant White.

Repeating Crosses, page 98: designed and pieced by Helen Whitson Rose; quilted by Millie Atkins.

Indian Trails, pages 74 and 101: designed by Susan Ramey Wright; made by Annie C. Phillips.

Stars Over My Garden Maze, pages 106 and 110: designed and made by Arleen Boyd.

Starry Angels Wall Quilt, page 113, and **Christmas Pillows,** pages 113 and 115: designed and made by Cynthia Moody Wheeler.

Stepping Stones, pages 118 and 120: designed and made by Annie C. Phillips. Sled from Huffstutler's Hardware, Homewood, Alabama.

Black Tie Affair, pages 123 and 124: designed and made by Pamla P. Johnson. Top hat and gloves from Mr. Burch Formal Wear, Mountain Brook, Alabama.

Winter Roses, page 128: designed by Susan Ramey Wright; made by Irene Frederick.

Amethyst, pages 132 and 142: designed by Susan Ramey Wright; made by Mary Ramey.

In the Bleak Midwinter, pages 104, 135, and 137: designed by Susan Ramey Wright; made by Judy Cantwell.

Snowy, Snowy Night, page 138: designed by Susan Ramey Wright; pieced by Mary Ramey; quilted by Performance Resources, Inc.

Special thanks to the following for sharing their homes, businesses, and resources in the production of photography in this book: Birmingham Botanical Gardens; Constitution Hall Village; Jack E. Crouch; Pride Fisher; Sara and Don Gohr; Sue and Buck Haddock; Homestead Hollow; Alice and Ben Johnson; Prudence and Robert Johnson; Kimberly Clark Corporation; La Paz Mexican Restaurant; Lake Purdy Boat Landing; Kit Samford; Barbara Stone; Sugar Creek Orchards Farmer's Market; Mr. and Mrs. Louis Wilhite.

Quilts in this book were made with batting provided by the following companies:

American Fiber Industries (Crafter's Cabin)
689 Mesquit Street
Los Angeles, CA 90021

Fairfield Processing (Polyfil)
P.O. Box 1130
Danbury, CT 06813

Hobbs Bonded Fibers (Polydown)
Craft Products Division
P.O. Box 3000
Mexia, TX 76667

Stearns Technical Textiles Co. (Mountain Mist)
100 Williams Street
Cincinnati, OH 45215

Warm Products, Inc. (Warm & Natural)
16120 Woodinville-Redmond Rd. #5
Woodinville, WA 98072

How to Improve Your Quilting Stitch by Ami Simms is available for $6.95 plus $1.50 shipping from Mallery Press, 4206 Sheraton Drive, Flint, MI 48532-3557.